DISCOVERING
GRIFFITH PARK

DISCOVERING GRIFFITH PARK
A LOCAL'S GUIDE

CASEY SCHREINER

MOUNTAINEERS
BOOKS

For my partner, Daniel Lyman, who was the first person to encourage me to give Griffith Park's trails a closer look

MOUNTAINEERS BOOKS is dedicated to the exploration, preservation, and enjoyment of outdoor and wilderness areas.

1001 SW Klickitat Way, Suite 201, Seattle, WA 98134
800-553-4453, www.mountaineersbooks.org

Printed in Korea
Distributed in the United Kingdom by Cordee, www.cordee.co.uk
First edition, 2020

Copyeditor: Ali Shaw
Design: Jen Grable
Cover Illustration and Layout: Kate Basart/Union Pageworks
Cartographer: Lohnes+Wright
All photographs by the author unless credited otherwise

Library of Congress Cataloging-in-Publication Data is on file for this title.

Mountaineers Books titles may be purchased for corporate, educational, or other promotional sales, and our authors are available for a wide range of events. For information on special discounts or booking an author, contact our customer service at 800-553-4453 or mbooks@mountaineersbooks.org.

Printed on FSC®-certified materials

ISBN (paperback): 978-1-68051-266-3
ISBN (ebook): 978-1-68051-267-0

An independent nonprofit publisher since 1960

Contents

HOW DO I SEE THE HOLLYWOOD SIGN? 41

OTHER OUTDOOR STUFF 49

MUSEUMS AND CULTURAL ATTRACTIONS 77

HIKING IN GRIFFITH PARK 93

Land Acknowledgment

We
The Indigenous People
The Traditional Caretakers of this landscape
are the direct descendants of the First People who formed our lands
our worlds during creation time.
We have always been here.
Our Ancestors prepared and became the landscapes and worlds
for the coming of humans with order/knowledge and gifts
embedded in the landscape.
Our Ancestors, imbued the responsibility and obligation to our original
instructions, guided by protocol and etiquette to be part of, take care of,
and ensure the welfare of the extended family and community
defined its most inclusive expression, the NATURE
and to pass those teachings and responsibilities onto our children,
grandchildren and many generations to come.
(AND to all those that now live here).

—Tongva land acknowledgment for the land
now known as Griffith Park provided by
Julia Bogany, cultural officer of the Tongva Tribe

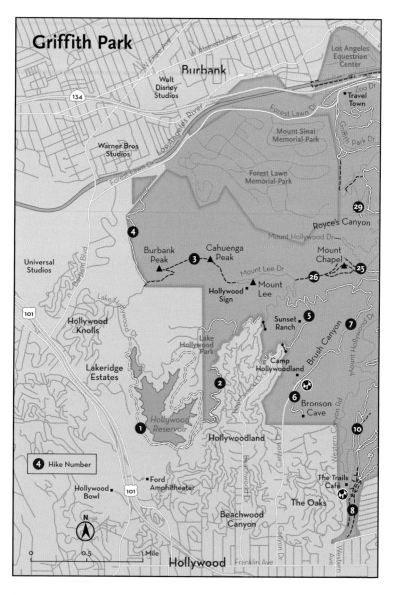

Griffith Park

Burbank

Los Angeles Equestrian Center

Walt Disney Studios

134

Zoo Dr

Travel Town

Forest Lawn Dr

Mount Sinai Memorial-Park

Warner Bros Studios

Forest Lawn Dr

Los Angeles River

Griffith Park Dr

Forest Lawn Memorial-Park

29

Royce's Canyon

Mount Hollywood Dr

Universal Studios

Burbank Peak

Cahuenga Peak

Mount Chapel

25

N Barham Blvd

3

Mount Lee Dr

26

101

Lake Hollywood Dr

Mount Lee

Hollywood Sign

Hollywood Knolls

Lake Hollywood Park

Sunset Ranch

5

Brush Canyon

7

Mount Hollywood Dr

Lakeridge Estates

2

Camp Hollywoodland

6

Bronson Cave

Beachwood Dr

Western Canyon Rd

1

Hollywood Reservoir

Hollywoodland

10

4 Hike Number

Canyon Dr

Ford Amphitheater

The Trails Café

Hollywood Bowl

101

The Oaks

8

N

Beachwood Canyon

Canyon Dr

Western Ave

0   0.5   1 Mile

Hollywood   Franklin Ave

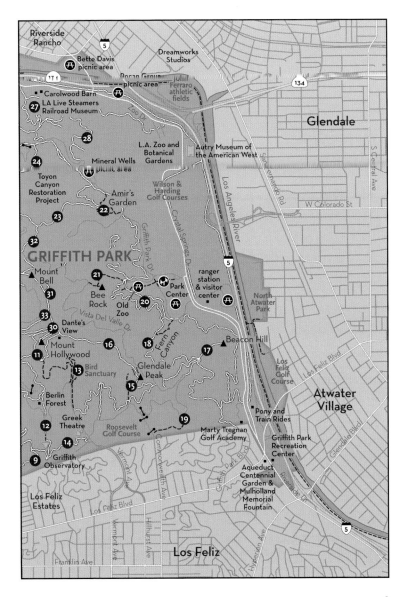

Riverside
Rancho

Bette Davis
picnic area

Dreamworks
Studios

Carolwood Barn

27 LA Live Steamers
Railroad Museum

28

24

Toyon
Canyon
Restoration
Project

23

32

GRIFFITH PARK

Mount
Bell

31

33

30

Dante's
View

11

Mount
Hollywood

13

Bird
Sanctuary

Berlin
Forest

12

Greek
Theatre

14

9

Griffith
Observatory

Los Feliz
Estates

Pecan Grove
picnic area

Ferraro
athletic
fields

Zoo Dr

L.A. Zoo and
Botanical
Gardens

Autry Museum of
the American West

Mineral Wells
picnic area

Amir's
Garden

22

Griffith Park Dr

Crystal Springs Dr

Wilson &
Harding
Golf Courses

Los Angeles River

San Fernando Rd

21

Bee
Rock

Old
Zoo

20

Vista Del Valle Dr

16

18

Fern Canyon

17

Park
Center

ranger
station
& visitor
center

North
Atwater
Park

5

Beacon Hill

Glendale
Peak

15

Roosevelt
Golf Course

Commonwealth Ave

19

Marty Tregnan
Golf Academy

Pony and
Train Rides

Griffith Park Blvd

Griffith Park
Recreation
Center

Aqueduct
Centennial
Garden &
Mulholland
Memorial
Fountain

Vermont Ave

Hillhurst Ave

Los Feliz Blvd

Riverside Dr

Los Feliz

Glendale

S Central Ave

W Colorado St

Los Feliz
Golf
Course

**Atwater
Village**

Glendale Blvd

Hyperion Ave

Franklin Ave

Preface

Griffith Park is one of the wildest, largest, and most untamed parks in the US, and it sits smack in the middle of its second-largest city—a place that invented and exported urban-suburban sprawl, the freeway, and the auto-centric strip mall. In the region that brought us the four-level stack freeway interchange (still causing headaches at the junction of the 101 and 110), a mature male mountain lion has inspired activists to build the world's largest wildlife crossing at Liberty Canyon. Just above Hollywood Boulevard, where it's often easier to see a star on a sidewalk than in the night sky, one of the nation's oldest planetariums has been educating the public about our place in the cosmos for free for generations.

Millions of people have seen Griffith Park in films and television, but you'll still find longtime Los Angeles residents who have no idea where it is, what's in it, or how to get there. The park is home to the city's once-primary source of water—which was feared, then despised, then dammed and forced into a concrete tomb, only to be loved again and, in the future, set free. Even the story of the park's donor is one of contradictions, wrapped in scandal and philanthropy, attempted murder and inhuman generosity, regressive ideas about people and progressive ideas about parks.

In many ways, then, Griffith Park is a reflection of Los Angeles itself. It is both an urban oasis and an untamed wilderness, a manicured garden and smoldering chaparral slope. It is home to hikers, stargazers, cyclists, golfers, equestrians, train enthusiasts, Shakespearean actors, drum circles, museum patrons, kayakers, dog walkers, *people* walkers, environmentalists, developers, gardeners, charlatans, anarchic trail runners, secret handshake practitioners, ghost hunters, *eloteros*, zookeepers, dreamers, and everyone in between. I hope you have fun discovering it.

OPPOSITE: *Hikers enjoy a clear view of the Hollywood Sign on the Innsdale Trail* (Hike 2).

Griffith Park:
An Introduction

Although it's often compared to places like New York's Central Park or San Francisco's Golden Gate Park, Griffith Park is its own unique, *very* L.A. thing. First, it dwarfs those other famous parks—it's more than four times the size of Golden Gate and five times the size of Central Park. At over 4300 acres, Griffith Park is one of the largest municipal parks in North America.

Griffith is also much more rugged and wild than Golden Gate or Central. Located in the easternmost part of the Santa Monica Mountains, Griffith Park is home to rare chaparral, sage scrub, and oak woodlands with unique, endemic species of plants and animals—and a famous mountain lion, too. And it has all of that while also offering up more traditional developed park amenities like golf courses, a zoo, and an observatory you've definitely seen in the movies. Oh yeah, and there's a big sign you've probably seen before, too.

The park turns 125 years old in 2021 and gets more annual visitors than most national parks (over 12 million a year at last count!), but the book you're holding right now is the first in-depth guidebook written about it. Beyond all that, Griffith Park *deserves* its own book because it's weird, it's messy, it's complex, and it's wonderful. Incredible stories have happened here—and incredible things will happen here in the future.

This is not a completely comprehensive look at every nook and cranny of the park, nor is it an attempt to tell every tale within its borders. But you can consider this book a sort of "pocket visitor center" for the park. It's a way to make sense of the park depending on what you're looking to do and how you want to get around, and it will give you a sense of the park's history and place in Los Angeles. The park's major museums and attractions are

OPPOSITE: *Native oaks provide a welcome respite from the SoCal sun.*

described here as well as the unique gardens and monuments that have been special places for Angelenos and visitors for generations.

The book also details different uses for the park, including picnicking, cycling, horseback riding, and more, and provides maps that help you focus on the activities you want to enjoy.

Of course, there's also hiking here: I highlight thirty-three different routes in and around the park, from gentle walks you can do with a stroller to tough full-day adventures that will leave you exhausted and exhilarated.

And don't worry—I've got some good spots for Hollywood Sign selfies, too.

A BRIEF HISTORY OF THE LAND

Although the story of Griffith Park is often told in the scope of the timeline of the guy the park is named after, it should go without saying that the land that comprises Griffith Park existed long before Griffith J. Griffith set foot in the region.

The people who are today broadly known as the Tongva-Gabrielino (both the name and the spelling may vary) have thousands of years of history in Los Angeles County. Before Europeans arrived, this landscape would have looked significantly different—no manicured picnic areas or golf courses, but dense old-growth oak woodlands and sage scrub that supported large animals like grizzly bears. The Los Angeles River had no concrete boundaries, and it changed courses and directions often with the floodwaters and supported large fish like steelhead trout. And of course, the city's ubiquitous freeways weren't here—but you could still find travelers and traders tracing the future route of the 101 in the land known as Tovaangar, with villages stretching from present-day Santa Clarita to Palos Verdes and inland to the San Gabriel Mountains, western San Bernardino Valley, and Santiago Peak in northern Orange County.

Many findings are very new, but scholars now believe there were at least three Tongva-Gabrielino settlements in the vicinity of Griffith Park—one near Fern Dell, one west of Travel Town near Universal City, and one near where the Los Feliz adobe and ranger station are today.

The histories of the original inhabitants of this land—like many throughout the Americas—sadly were forgotten or actively erased by those who came later, but the descendants of those original people still live here. Indeed, Los Angeles is the city with the second-highest number of Native American citizens in the country, and thankfully there is a renewed interest and attempt to preserve and tell their stories. The Autry Museum inside Griffith Park continues to break new ground in bringing these histories back to life with a combination of scholarly research and personal outreach to modern Tongva-Gabrielino representatives

The first known recorded instances of Europeans inside Griffith Park came with Juan Bautista de Anza's 1775–76 expedition to establish an overland route from Sonora, Mexico, to Monterey, then the capital of Alta California. Anza brought 240 colonists and 40 soldiers on this 1200-mile trek. Their journey took them along the Los Angeles River in what is now Griffith Park, and there is record of the party camping there, although it's not clear exactly where—some scholars think it was near today's John Ferraro athletic fields; a plaque near the Pecan Grove picnic area commemorates the expedition.

One of the soldiers in the Anza expedition was José Vicente Feliz, who returned to Los Angeles in 1781 as the military leader of Los Pobladores—the original forty-four settlers and four soldiers who walked from Sinaloa and Sonora, Mexico, to found *El Pueblo de la Reina de Los Ángeles Sobre el Río de la Porciúncula* ("The Town of the Queen of Angels on the River Porciúncula"—think about *that* the next time someone complains about people shortening the full name of the city to "L.A."). This event is commemorated on Labor Day weekend with processions, Masses, and a celebration usually held in the Pueblo de Los Angeles at Olvera Street.

Feliz spent some time in San Diego but returned to the Pueblo in 1787 to serve as the governor's representative. For his efforts, he was given a Spanish land grant from Cahuenga Pass to the Los Angeles River, including much of the flatlands to the south. The land became known as Rancho Los Feliz.

Feliz died in 1822—one year after Mexico won its independence from Spain. His daughter-in-law Doña María Ygnacia Verdugo took over the operations of Rancho Los Feliz and immediately exercised some pretty sharp business and legal acumen during a period of relative instability in the region. She registered a lucrative personal cattle brand, successfully petitioned the new Mexican government for a confirmation of her land rights to Rancho Los Feliz, and—perhaps most importantly—secured the rancho's water rights to the Los Angeles River.

The next few decades were tumultuous for both the Los Feliz estate and for California in general. Throughout the 1830s and '40s, tension mounted between Californios and Mexicans, and eventually between Mexico and the United States, culminating in the Mexican-American War from 1846 to 1848. Even before California became part of the United States, American businessmen were moving into the region and taking advantage of the messy legal paperwork to basically seize rancho land. Doña María's ironclad contracts kept most of them at bay, but by the 1850s she had sold off sections of the rancho to her daughters and passed the bulk of Rancho Los Feliz to her son Antonio, who would build the still-standing walls of the Los Feliz adobe house in 1853 (today, it's the Park Film Office).

THE CURSE OF THE FELIZES

One of the best-known and most-told ghost stories in Griffith Park is the so called Curse of the Felizes. According to legend, Don Antonio Feliz—then the bachelor landowner of Rancho Los Feliz—succumbed to a smallpox outbreak in 1863. Before he died, he sent his young niece Petranilla away to prevent infection while his sister Soledad stayed on.

When Petranilla was away, Don Antonio signed a deathbed will witnessed by his friend Antonio Coronel and an unnamed lawyer. Soledad got some furniture. Petranilla got a big fat nothing. And Coronel, by some strange stroke of luck, got all of Rancho Los Feliz.

It's understandable, then, that Petranilla was a bit peeved when she returned to find her home no longer in the hands of her family. This is when she apparently cursed anyone who owned the land that rightfully belonged to the Feliz family, at least according to notorious yarn spinner Horace Bell. Local historian and outdoor author John W. Robinson dug into this legend in the 1980s and essentially said Bell made the whole thing up.

Misfortune did seem to be a regular occurrence at Rancho Los Feliz from then onward, though. Coronel quickly gave all the land to his lawyer, who was later shot and killed. Next up was Leon Baldwin, whose crops failed and cattle died, forcing him to sell to Griffith J. Griffith. Baldwin was later murdered by bandits in Mexico, and Griffith experienced his own series of unfortunate events, too. The ghosts of Don Antonio and Petranilla have both allegedly been seen at Bee Rock and at the old Feliz adobe but have reportedly calmed down now that the land is a public park.

Unfortunately, Antonio didn't have as much luck with the rancho as his mom did. A combination of a smallpox outbreak and some shenanigans from Yankee lawyers brought the land into American hands and eventually to the park's namesake, Griffith J. Griffith.

The Complicated Story of Griffith J. Griffith

Born in 1850 in South Wales (where, apparently, it's not uncommon for people to have the same first and last name) to a large, poor, Protestant family, Griffith Jenkins Griffith lived in the same stone house that had been in his family for generations. His parents divorced after he was born, but he ended up sharing this farmhouse with five half brothers and three half sisters.

As a young boy Griffith lived with various relatives throughout this coal- and iron-mining region of Wales until an uncle offered to take him to America. He moved to Pennsylvania at the age of sixteen and became the de facto adopted son of the Mowry family, who had lost their son in the Civil War.

Griffith made a name for himself with his writing—first working for the Pennsylvania Brewers Association and later as a reporter for the *Daily Alta California* in the 1870s. Griffith talked up his experience living near the mines in Wales and became the region's first mining correspondent. This job saw him traveling across the Southwest and into Mexico—and put him in touch with some of the richest and most powerful people, too.

Griffith's journalism transitioned into more lucrative mining boosterism and eventually into investment in mines, where he undoubtedly had a lot of access to insider information from his writing contacts. Griffith made enough money to purchase 4071 acres of Rancho Los Feliz in 1882.

He made more money through lending and real estate—and started making enemies in Los Angeles with his somewhat ostentatious behavior. He adopted the title of Colonel (despite never actually achieving that rank in a military outfit) and was known to parade around downtown in long overcoats with an exquisite gold-headed cane, earning the ire of some of the city's stuffiest shirts. At the same time, though, Griffith was active in philanthropy, both personal and civic—on a trip to Europe he paid for his father and eight siblings to come to America and put the youngest through school. He also paid for the Mowrys' living expenses after they fell on tough times and built them an

GHOSTS OF GRIFFITH PARK

The Curse of the Felizes isn't the only ghost story told in Griffith Park. The ghost of Peg Entwistle is said to haunt the southern flank of Mount Lee. The struggling actress moved to a house on Beachwood Drive for a fresh start in Hollywood, but the film that was supposed to be her big break ended up bombing. On September 18, 1932, she climbed to the top of the *H* in the Hollywoodland Sign and jumped off, killing herself. Paranormal-minded hikers have claimed to see her falling from the *H* or wandering the nearby trails at night, and they often report the scent of her favorite gardenia perfume in the air.

Interestingly enough, the number of ghost stories and sightings in Griffith Park increased exponentially once the internet came around. Of these, Haunted Picnic Table 29 is perhaps the best known. In 2006, an *L.A. Times* article appeared online detailing a freakish accident that supposedly occurred north of Mount Chapel on Mount Hollywood Drive, where thirty years prior, a young couple was crushed by a falling tree while making love on a picnic table. Workers who tried to clear the tree fell ill, including a supervisor who suffered a heart attack. Although the article was a hoax (the URL for the still-online website reads "www.latirnes.com," the column is written by "Norm Bates," and photos are credited to "Michael Myers" and "Art Banksy"), that hasn't stopped people from searching out the site (it has an official location on Google Maps) or reporting additional sightings.

Actress Peg Entwislle in 1925 (Theatrical Portrait Photographs, TCS 28, Harvard Theatre Collection, Houghton Library, Harvard University)

Other hauntings in the park include ghost tigers in the Old L.A. Zoo, disappearing people at the merry-go-round and Griffith Observatory, phantom trains at Travel Town, and something known as "the Griffith Park Creature." As the years go on and more imaginative folks move to L.A. from all over the world, you can expect even more ghost stories to pop up, but I think the best way to see ghosts in the park is to enjoy some of the real-life Halloween seasonal attractions like Boney Island, the Haunted Hayride, and the Halloween Ghost Train.

exquisite gravestone marker. And remember Doña Verdugo's hard-fought water rights? Griffith sold them to the downstream city for *well* below market value, becoming a bona fide hero to the thirsty boomtown.

Griffith wooed and wedded Mary Agnes Christina Mesmer (often known as Tina) in 1887, had one son named Van, and turned his attention to the future of Los Angeles. When he toured Europe, he noticed that all the major cities also had major parks. Even in the growing cities of the United States, parks were an important part of civic pride—but in his adopted Los Angeles, the park situation was pretty poor. So on December 16, 1896, Griffith and Tina presented 3015 acres of Rancho Los Feliz to the City of Los Angeles as a Christmas present explicitly for use as a public park, essentially giving the town a park four times the size of New York City's Central Park overnight. An engraved copy of the deed is visible in the Griffith Park Visitor Center.

The public's love and admiration for Griffith was relatively short-lived—on September 3, 1903, the publicly teetotaling Griffith stumbled into the presidential suite of Santa Monica's Hotel Arcadia, drunk. He accused his Catholic wife of trying to poison him on behalf of the pope and shot her in the face with a revolver.

Miraculously, she survived and escaped by jumping out a window to the nearby owner's suite. The fallout was immediate—Griffith was shunned from society and became entangled in one of L.A.'s earliest celebrity trials. His lawyers used a defense of "alcoholic insanity," and he spent two years in San Quentin Prison and paid a fine of $5000. Understandably, Tina got a divorce.

The City of Los Angeles didn't want much to do with Griffith after this episode, although he continued to donate land for parks and money for an observatory and a Greek-style theater inside the park that bore his name. In his

"Colonel" Griffith Jenkins Griffith, 1903 (University of Southern California Libraries, California Historical Society)

1910 book *Parks, Boulevards, and Playgrounds*, Griffith laid out some fairly progressive ideas about city parks, including the notion that they should be free to everyone so as not to become the playgrounds of the rich. He also wrote that cities had an obligation to provide public transportation to the parks so everyone could access them—issues we are still dealing with more than a hundred years later. (He walked the walk on this, too—at various times, both Griffith and his son, Van, personally ran their own bus lines into the park when the City refused.) In that book, though, Griffith was also prickly about being excluded from society life and euphemistically described his prison time as "my forced absence from the city," so . . . we can't say he was totally repentant about the whole shooting-his-wife-in-the-face thing either.

Griffith died on July 6, 1919, embroiled in a court battle with a parks commission that didn't want to accept his donations for the theater and observatory. He left the money for the park in his will as the Griffith J. Griffith Charitable Trust, which continues to actively fight for the preservation, protection, and improvement of the park today. Griffith J. Griffith is buried in the Hollywood Forever Cemetery on Santa Monica Boulevard.

FLORA AND FAUNA

Visitors fighting their way through the "concrete jungle" of Los Angeles are often surprised to see the vast array of wild plant and animal life that makes its home in Griffith Park. The most commonly seen mammals are mule deer, squirrels, and coyotes, although it is not uncommon to run into raccoons, opossums, rabbits, and skunks on the trails as well. Quiet and lucky visitors may be blessed with a glimpse of a bobcat (it took me years of hiking here before I spotted one while writing this book). In 2012, researchers discovered a male mountain lion, now known as P-22, living inside Griffith Park—you will most likely never see him, but if you come across tracks, consider yourself extremely lucky!

A number of lizards and snakes make their home in Griffith Park, too—you will most often encounter alligator lizards and western fence lizards in the park (the western fence lizards are the ones that look like they're doing push-ups; alligator lizards are more commonly found near water sources). These lizards often have a habit of bolting through the brush while you're hiking nearby, spooking you into thinking something more dangerous is around.

An L.A. Conservation Corps worker helps an alligator lizard find its way back to the Los Angeles River.

During the wet season, you may also get to see (or hear) western toads near creeks, arroyos, or the Los Angeles River. Most snakes that live inside the park are harmless, but the Southern Pacific rattlesnake is here as well and should be treated with caution (more on that in a bit).

Bug lovers will enjoy walking the paths and trails of the parks, where they're almost guaranteed to see at least a stink beetle showing off its good side to humans. Praying mantises will often hang out hoping to catch a meal on branches; numerous moths and butterflies can be found depending on the season; and there's a common, slow-moving insect with the wonderful name of diabolical ironclad beetle—known as the tank of the insect world.

Tarantulas are known to hike the trails at sunset during their mating season. These arachnids only bite in self-defense, and their venom is weaker than that of a typical bee. They burrow underground and are very sensitive to the vibration of the ground—for example, from passing feet, wheels, or hooves.

If you're not a birder, Griffith Park may inspire you to become one. More than two hundred species of birds have been identified in the park, which is both a wintering home for many species and a pit stop on migration paths. The range of birds here is impressive—crows and ravens swipe goodies from picnickers; great blue herons slowly stalk the Los Angeles River looking for

Tarantulas may inspire fear, but they're pretty harmless to humans. (photo by Raphael Mazor)

frogs and fish to eat; majestic birds of prey like red-tailed hawks, Cooper's hawks, and peregrine falcons soar on thermals far above the park; Anna's and Allen's hummingbirds zip through the chaparral sipping nectar; mockingbirds and black-headed grosbeaks fill the air with song (a great reason to leave those headphones and speakers at home); acorn woodpeckers fill up trees with future meals; and California scrub jays can sometimes be spotted darting to and from their food caches—research has shown they can remember up to two hundred storage locations, along with what's stored inside and how quickly it's decaying.

The main plant communities found in Griffith Park are coastal sage scrub and chaparral. I've used this joke before, but there's an easy way to tell the difference: If you smell nice, you're in sage scrub. If you're bleeding, you're in chaparral.

Both communities are dominated by low-growing, brushy shrubs. Sage scrub, as the name would imply, features fragrant but unassuming California sagebrush (often called "cowboy cologne") along with various species of sage like black and white sage. California buckwheats—which flower through much of the year—are common, and California brittlebush puts on a bright yellow sunflowerlike display in the early spring. Larger shrubs include leafy toyon and lemonade berry as well as ceanothus.

Chaparral is often mixed in along with sage scrub (if you want to get *super* technical, we're in a subecoregion of the California chaparral and woodlands ecoregion called the California coastal sage and chaparral ecoregion), but generally the plants in chaparral are tougher, need less water, and are more likely to poke you with something. You can usually find these plants on the sunnier

COULD IT HAVE BEEN TOYONWOOD?

An oft-repeated but most likely apocryphal story about how Hollywood got its name goes like this: There are large bushes growing all over the Santa Monica Mountains here that produce showy red berries in late fall and early winter. *Heteromeles arbutifolia* is commonly known as toyon, but to the swarms of new residents coming to Los Angeles from the East, the plant looked enough like holly to be called California holly or Christmas berry. A lot of holly here, therefore, Hollywood. Sounds good, right?

That origin of Hollywood has been attributed to Daeida Wilcox Beveridge. If you start digging into it, you'll find Beveridge is also the source of about a half dozen alternate origins for the name, too. There's more evidence that Beveridge got the name from her neighbor Ivar Weid, who lived in what he called Holly Canyon . . . which, actually, might have been named after those toyon after all. As they say, "This is the West—when the legend becomes fact, print the legend."

No matter where the name came from, toyon is still plentiful in the hills of Griffith Park, and its bright red berries are a clear indicator that winter is on its way. Toyon is also the only California native plant to retain its indigenous name (from the Bay Area Ohlone people) and makes a wonderful drought-tolerant evergreen shrub, providing food and habitat to dozens of species throughout the year. Toyon was named the official plant of Los Angeles in 2012.

When its berries are present, toyon is easy to spot on the hills around Los Angeles.

ABOVE: *Purple sage (Salvia leucophylla) blooms at different elevations for months, while delicate mariposa lilies (genus Calochortus) are more elusive.*
BELOW: *Southern bush monkeyflower (Diplacus longiflorus) explodes with color in late spring.*

south-facing slopes in the park. Prickly pear cactus can be found here, along with Shaw's agave and otherworldly *Dudleya* species, chamise, manzanita, and yucca.

Both plant communities feature a variety of endemic trees, including coast live oaks, western sycamores (which lose their leaves in the early winter, giving us a tiny taste of fall), and rare California black walnut trees, which are found only in the L.A. area.

Because Griffith Park has had a lot of different caretakers—and they haven't always been mindful of native species—there are also many introduced and invasive species that have found their way into the park.

Community Science

One of the most exciting and effective ways of learning how to identify the flora and fauna you spot in Griffith Park—and anywhere, really—is by engaging in community science. Sometimes called "citizen science," *community science* is the term for when scientists work with us regular folks to gather and interpret data about the world around us.

LEARNING MORE ABOUT WHAT'S AROUND

Interested in learning more about the flora and fauna nearby? Both the L.A. Zoo and Autry Museum inside the park are great places to start. If you'd like to learn even more, I recommend two must-visit destinations: For plants, the Theodore Payne Foundation in Sun Valley features an extensive nursery of California native plants as well as demonstration gardens and classes. The grounds are located at 10459 Tuxford Street in Sun Valley. Call 818-768-1802 or visit www.theodorepayne.org for more info.

Likewise, the Natural History Museum of Los Angeles County has done an incredible job over the past few years of making nature come alive for city dwellers. They have an accessible and informative permanent *Nature Lab* exhibit about the wildlife present in Southern California; their native and edible garden will help you identify plants you see out in the wild and give you ideas for your own garden; and they have a variety of programs both on-site and in the field, including bioblitz days. The museum is located at 900 West Exposition Boulevard in Los Angeles. Call 213-763-3466 or visit https://nhm.org for information and exhibits.

FAMOUS ANIMALS OF GRIFFITH PARK

Griffith Park's history with famous critters arguably begins in the 1950s, when a kangaroo named Parky walked the grounds on weekends with a pith-helmeted ranger who handed out park information and encouraged visitors not to litter. At the same time, the much-criticized Griffith Park Zoo had an *in*famous resident named Ivan the Terrible—a nine-hundred-pound male polar bear who killed three other polar bears in the zoo and was generally feared by everyone in Los Angeles.

But the area has had some more recent, friendlier famous animals, including Reggie the Alligator, who was illegally raised in captivity and released in Harbor City in 2005. He was spotted in a lake there for several years and became a media sensation before being captured in 2007 and moved to the L.A. Zoo. Later that year, Reggie escaped his habitat and was found soaking up some rays near the loading dock. He still resides in the zoo today.

The L.A. Zoo's most recent famous addition is Hope, a California condor. Hope was hatched in captivity in Idaho and was meant to be released into the wild as part of a rehabilitation effort for the species, but when they noticed she had a wing injury, she was instead moved to the L.A. Zoo, where she now serves as an educational ambassador and the world's first California condor to participate in a free-flight bird show.

Arguably the most famous animal inside Griffith Park, however, is the male mountain lion known as P-22. First discovered on wildlife cameras by Angeleno biologist Miguel Ordeñana in 2012, P-22 has become something of a mascot for the cause of urban wildlife in L.A. To reach Griffith Park, P-22 had to cross the 101 and I-405, two of the nation's largest and busiest freeways. He has helped Angelenos become more aware of the dangers of rodenticide, more appreciative of the natural world in their city, and more generous toward an ambitious project to build the world's largest wildlife crossing over the 101 at Liberty Canyon. He even has his own Facebook page and Instagram account (www.facebook.com/p22mountainlionof hollywood and www.instagram.com/p22mountainlion, respectively), and he remains a beloved citizen of Los Angeles . . . even after he allegedly popped into the L.A. Zoo in 2016 to snack on a koala bear.

Over the past few years, this data gathering and interpretation has been made exponentially easier with the development of free smartphone apps like iNaturalist (www.inaturalist.org). When you take a photo of something with your smartphone, it will usually automatically assign it a time stamp and geo-location. When you get home, you can upload those photos via the app or website, and other community members will help you identify what you saw. Then scientists can use that data to help track migrations, invasive species, the effects of climate change, and other information—and you'll have fun learning about what you saw, too.

Dangerous Stuff
Most accidents in Griffith Park are usually the result of underestimating a hike, not taking enough food or water, or spending too much time outside when it's hot. Animal encounters are extremely rare, and most are easily avoidable, as the majority of healthy animals want absolutely nothing to do with humans.

Coyotes
Coyotes are the largest animal you're most likely to encounter in the park. Coyotes have had a negative stigma for generations, but these expert survivors have adapted well to the urban landscape of Griffith Park. They will generally

A coyote (Canis latrans) searches among California sagebrush and buckwheat. (photo by Sarah Brewer)

P-22 has a solid claim on being the most famous mountain lion (Puma concolor) *in the world.* (photo by Miguel Ordeñana)

leave you alone, but take care with small children and dogs—there's a reason dogs are required to be on leash everywhere inside the park!

If you encounter a coyote or pack of coyotes and they don't seem to be moving away on their own, the advice is the same as for most larger animals—stand your ground and make a lot of noise. They'll usually look at you oddly and duck back into the brush.

Mountain Lions

There is exactly one known mountain lion living inside Griffith Park, P-22, and he is collared and tracked. Although P-22's range is significantly smaller than that of other mountain lions, his behavior hasn't changed much—he's extremely elusive, hunts by stealth, and actively avoids human encounters.

If you do encounter P-22—or any other mountain lion—stay calm and consider yourself lucky. Mountain lion encounters statewide are extremely rare and even more rarely result in injury to humans. However, small animals and children may be at greater risk than adults. Just in case you do meet one, here are some tips, which are all generally good advice for any wildlife encounter you'd prefer to avoid:

- **Don't run:** Running may trigger the lion's hunting instinct and cause an encounter that may not otherwise happen.
- **Look big:** Mountain lions generally only attack prey that's smaller and weaker than they are. If you look large and aggressive, they'll back away. Stand up, open your jacket, and make a lot of noise.
- **Create distance:** While maintaining eye contact and making noise, slowly back away to give the lion space and an opportunity to escape. Remember not to turn your back, as that may trigger the lion's hunting instinct.

Rattlesnakes

There are several species of snake that live in Griffith Park, and venomous Southern Pacific rattlesnakes are among them. As with the other animals here, rattlesnakes generally don't want to see you as much as you don't want to see them, but sometimes an accidental encounter can turn dangerous.

You can avoid getting a snakebite by:

- **Wearing the right clothes:** Don't hike in flip-flops or open-toed shoes, and if you can, wear high boots and loose, long pants (which will also help protect you from the next critter I describe).
- **Staying on the trail:** Avoid tall, grassy areas where snakes may lounge during the day.
- **Using trekking poles:** Poles create extra vibrations on the ground that let snakes know something big is coming their way.

If you do happen to come across a snake on the trail, back away to give it room. Many snakes sense vibrations on the ground, so stomping around a bit may encourage it to move along without incident.

If you get bitten, stay calm, remove rings, watches, or any other items that may restrict swelling, and immobilize the bite area if you can. Contact the rangers at 323-644-6661 or call 911.

Ticks

On the more popular trails in Griffith Park, the wide paths and frequent foot traffic mean you're not especially likely to encounter ticks—but they are here. If you find yourself deeper in the backcountry or hiking through an overgrown area, it's worth your time to stop for a quick tick check afterward, especially in the warmer summer and fall months.

The best way to avoid a tick bite is to make it more difficult for them to get to you. Wear long sleeves and pants and light-colored clothing and tuck your pants into your socks if you don't mind getting a citation from the fashion police. If you do get bitten by a tick, it's gross but relatively easy to remove it with a pair of tweezers or a tick-removal tool. If you don't have one of those available, you can wait until you get home or go to a walk-in clinic instead—even if the tick is carrying pathogens, most of the ones they transmit generally won't enter your bloodstream until the tick has been attached for at least twenty-four hours.

Do not attempt to remove the tick by pulling on it with your fingers, putting rubbing alcohol on it, setting it on fire, or doing anything else.

Poison Oak

Often spotted in shadier areas and along canyon floors and arroyos, poison oak is common and widespread throughout Griffith Park as both a climbing vine and a short shrub. That old rhyming rule "leaves of three, let it be" stands true here. Every part of this plant—including the leafless branches—contains an oil (urushiol) that can cause itchy rashes on the skin. Symptoms last one

A bane of hikers everywhere, poison oak (Toxicodendron diversilobum) *is present throughout Griffith Park.*

When the marine layer sits atop the L.A. basin, expect (and enjoy!) cool, gray mornings.

to two weeks and can be treated with topical lotions, aloe vera, and antihistamines. Note that the oil can stick around on dogs, horses, or even clothing items, so if you think you came across some on your trip, it's probably worth giving everything a good, thorough wash.

CLIMATE AND SEASONS

Newcomers and transplants are often confused and disappointed when they arrive and don't get their distinct spring-summer-fall-winter rotations. The reality is, Los Angeles does have very clear seasons, but they're more subtle than in other parts of the country. Spend some time here, though, and you'll learn to read the changes in the weather and landscape, too.

Although L.A.'s image is often one of perpetual, perfect blue skies, visitors in the "June Gloom" season (which can also manifest itself as "May Gray," "No-Sky July," or "Fogust") will be met by a low, dense marine layer of clouds off the Pacific Ocean that blankets much of the L.A. basin each morning through midafternoon. While those clouds may disappoint summer tourists, they provide welcome relief from brutal temperatures and can allow for tough midday hikes you wouldn't be able to do later in the season.

10 FUN FACTS
ABOUT GRIFFITH PARK

1 At over 4300 acres, Griffith Park is four times the size of San Francisco's Golden Gate Park and five times the size of New York's Central Park.

2 Griffith J. Griffith and his wife Mary Agnes Christina (Tina) Mesmer donated 3015 acres of Rancho Los Feliz to the City of Los Angeles as a Christmas gift on December 16, 1896. When the land was donated, the park was a mile north of the city limits of Los Angeles.

3 The original Hollywood Sign was built on Mount Lee in 1923, and read "Hollywoodland" to advertise a nearby housing development. It was expected to last only 18 months.

4 The Griffith Observatory opened in 1935 and is the most visited public observatory in the world. It is estimated that more people have looked through its Zeiss 12-inch refracting telescope than any other telescope in history.

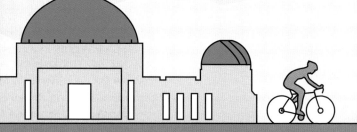

5 The oldest building in the park, the Park Film Office, is the only surviving building from Rancho Los Feliz. Its exterior adobe walls date from 1853.

6 Griffith Park is said to have inspired Walt Disney to create Disneyland. The innovative animator often spent time with his children at the circa-1926 merry-go-round.

7 Long a land of many uses, the park has been home to an airfield, multiple zoos, a landfill, a Civilian Conservation Corps work camp, a pre-internment camp and prisoner-of-war camp during World War II, housing for veterans, and more.

8 Griffith Park contains five museums: the Los Angeles Zoo and Botanical Gardens, the Autry Museum of the American West, the Griffith Observatory, Travel Town, and the Los Angeles Live Steamers Railroad Museum.

9 Griffith Park has been the site of countless films and television shows since its very beginning. Popular filming locations include the Bronson Cave, Cedar Grove, and the closed-to-traffic Mount Hollywood and Vista Del Valle Drives.

10 Griffith Park is home to hundreds of species of plants and animals ranging from carp in the L.A. River to a famous mountain lion named P-22 in the rugged chaparral.

HOLLYWOOD

The visitor center features beautiful artwork detailing the park history.

By June or July, the "Endless Summer" usually kicks in—and can sometimes last through November and even December, when you will be begging any higher power you believe in for sweet, sweet relief. During this time, the marine layer weakens, the temperatures rise, and many native plants go into summer dormancy (I sometimes call this "Summer Brown"). Hikers during these months should watch the forecasts and start early or wait until the sun is setting to hit the trails. Bring extra water, slather on the sunscreen, and pay attention for red-flag warnings and news of Santa Ana winds—dry, hot, often violent gusts that can knock down trees and powerlines, ignite and spread fires, and generally make everyone a bit crazier than usual.

Sometimes cooler days and light rain can sneak into October and November, but in general our "Winter-Spring" lasts from December to April, when the region gets 86 percent of our annual rainfall (on average, L.A. gets about 15 inches of rain a year—don't let anyone tell you it's a desert, OK?). These rainstorms can often be very heavy. I don't recommend hiking during a rainstorm but I *absolutely* recommend hiking the few days following one. Then, the skies clear and our native plants turn bright green and begin to bloom, making for unforgettable outdoor experiences.

GENERAL PARK RULES AND REGULATIONS
Almost everything inside this book is inside the boundaries of Griffith Park, which means these rules apply throughout. Where rules differ, they will be noted. In general:

- Fires and fireworks are prohibited everywhere in the park. Cooking should be done only in designated barbecue pits in picnic areas.
- Do not feed or bother wildlife of any kind.
- Collection or removal of any material inside the park is prohibited—this includes rocks, wildflowers, and artifacts.
- Dogs must be on leash at all times in the park. The *only* off-leash area is the official dog park west of the Ferraro athletic fields.
- Bicycles are prohibited on trails inside Griffith Park; they are permitted only on paved roads.
- The speed limit throughout the park is 25 miles per hour.
- Alcohol and smoking, including e-cigarettes and vape pens, are prohibited.
- Park hours are 5:00 AM through 10:30 PM.
- In case of emergency, contact the park rangers at 323-644-6661 or call 911. For basic information, call the visitor center at 323-644-2050.
- For the 2016 Cartifact map, head to the Griffith Park Visitor Center at 4730 Crystal Springs Drive or visit www.laparks.org/griffithpark.

TRANSPORTATION
It's often been said that Griffith Park is the quintessential Los Angeles park "because you have to drive your car to get around it." And while at one time that may have been considered a good thing by L.A.'s autophilic population, younger Angelenos are starting to see the drawbacks of building an infrastructure with cars in mind first and every other mode of transportation or way of moving around relegated to an afterthought.

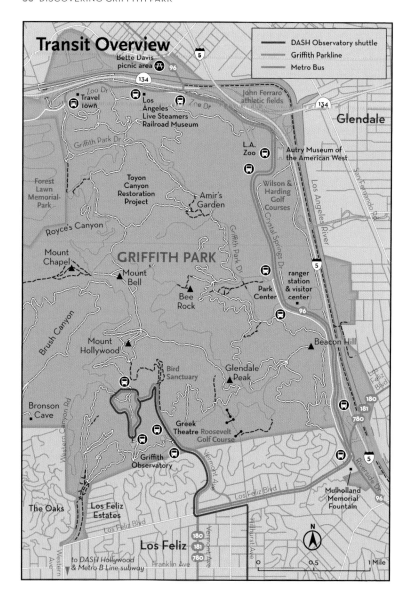

Transit Overview

Legend:
- DASH Observatory shuttle
- Griffith Parkline
- Metro Bus

Bette Davis picnic area — 96

Travel Town
Zoo Dr

Los Angeles Live Steamers Railroad Museum

Zoo Dr

John Ferraro athletic fields

Glendale

L.A. Zoo

Autry Museum of the American West

San Fernando Rd

Forest Lawn Memorial-Park

Toyon Canyon Restoration Project

Amir's Garden

Wilson & Harding Golf Courses

Los Angeles River

Royce's Canyon

Griffith Park Dr

Crystal Springs Dr

GRIFFITH PARK

Mount Chapel

Mount Bell

Bee Rock

Park Center

ranger station & visitor center

96

Brush Canyon

Mount Hollywood

Beacon Hill

Bronson Cave

Bird Sanctuary

Glendale Peak

Los Feliz Blvd

Western Canyon Rd

Greek Theatre

Roosevelt Golf Course

Vermont Ave

Griffith Observatory

Riverside Dr

The Oaks

Los Feliz Estates

Los Feliz Blvd

Mulholland Memorial Fountain

96

Los Feliz Blvd

Hillhurst Ave

Los Feliz

180 181 780

N

to DASH Hollywood & Metro B Line subway

Franklin Ave

Western Ave

0   0.5   1 Mile

THE MEANING OF NUMBERS

As you explore Griffith Park, you may begin to note that many objects in the park have numbers assigned to them. You will see numbers on water tanks, fire hydrants, and trail signs. This seemingly incomprehensible system can actually help you locate yourself—and more importantly, help rangers locate *you* in case of an emergency. If you need to contact the rangers, try to find a nearby trail sign, hydrant, or water tank and let them know what number it is—they'll know exactly where you are.

Also, there *is* a bit of rhyme and reason to the numbers on the water tanks—if you add a zero to the end of each number, that's the tank's elevation above sea level.

The numbered objects throughout the park help rangers find visitors quickly.

For such a large, heavily used, and much-loved park, it can still be frustrating to get around if you aren't driving your own car, but in the past few years both the city and the park have made great strides in making more parts of the park accessible by transit—and more improvements are on the way.

There are more and more ways to get around Griffith Park without a car.

DASH Shuttle

The DASH Observatory shuttle line run by the Los Angeles Department of Transportation (LADOT) is the easiest and most convenient way to access the often heavily congested area of Griffith Park between the Griffith Observatory and the Greek Theatre. Inside the park, this shuttle stops at both the observatory and the theater as well as at West Observatory Road/ Mount Hollywood Drive and at Commonwealth Canyon Drive, which means you can use this route to access many different hiking routes. The shuttle makes several stops in the Los Feliz neighborhood and connects with the Metro subway and Metro bus lines 2/302, 175, 304 and rapid lines 754 and 780 at Sunset Boulevard/ Vermont Avenue as well as Metro bus lines 180/181 at Vermont Avenue/Los Feliz Boulevard and 180/181 and the DASH Los Feliz line at Hillhurst Avenue/ Los Feliz Boulevard. Fare can be paid in exact change or with a Transit Access Pass (TAP) card, which can be purchased at any Metro subway station.

The DASH Hollywood shuttle stops at Franklin Avenue/Western Avenue in front of Immaculate Heart High School, which is a short 0.3-mile walk to the Fern Dell Drive entrance to the park.

For more information, including fares, timetables, and real-time updates, visit www.ladotbus.com and www.metro.net.

Metro Subway

Yes! L.A. does have a subway, and it comes *pretty* close to Griffith Park! The Metro B Line (formerly known as the Red Line) runs from North Hollywood to downtown Los Angeles, where it connects with the broader regional rail and rapid transit system. From the Hollywood/Western stop, you can reach the Fern Dell area of Griffith Park with an easy 0.6-mile walk north on Western Avenue. You can

Remember, the only place your pup can be off-leash in the park is in the dog park.

also connect to the DASH Observatory shuttle at the Vermont/Sunset stop. Fare includes transfers to other metro lines or buses within a two-hour window and is payable by TAP card, which can be purchased at any Metro subway station. For more information, timetables, and directions, visit www.metro.net.

Metro Buses

Metro runs 165 different bus routes with nearly 14,000 bus stops all over L.A. County. The system can be a bit daunting to navigate—especially if you don't have access to their online trip planner or a smartphone with online mapping—but once you get the hang of it, it's a great, cheap way to avoid dealing with parking and some traffic. Metro bus line 96 runs from the Burbank Amtrak station to downtown L.A. and through the eastern edge of Griffith Park. This line stops at the Bette Davis picnic area, Zoo Drive/Riverside Drive, the Autry Museum of the American West, the L.A. Zoo, Shane's Inspiration playground, the Griffith Park ranger station at Crystal Springs, the pony rides and Griffith Park & Southern Railroad, the corner of Los Feliz Boulevard and Riverside Drive near the Mulholland Memorial Fountain, Griffith Park pool and tennis courts, and the Friendship Auditorium. The line runs about once every hour.

The Griffith Parkline

In late 2019, Griffith Park launched an ambitious and much-needed pilot shuttle program called the Griffith Parkline. Running only on weekends (for now), the Griffith Parkline connects some of the most popular areas of the park without requiring a transfer—and admission is free. The shuttle runs from noon until 10:00 PM and has twelve stops, from Travel Town all the way to the Griffith Observatory. The Parkline allows visitors to explore the park without having to move their car (or even take a car into the park in the first place), and it also allows weekend hikers many more options for point-to-point hikes.

If the Parkline is successful, there are plans to increase its frequency, run it during the weekdays, and potentially even expand into other parts of the park.

OPPOSITE: *The Hollywood Sign isn't on Mount Hollywood, but that peak does have a nice view of it.*

How Do I See the Hollywood Sign?

Spend a little bit of time in Griffith Park—or heck, anywhere in L.A.—and eventually you'll hear The Question: "So how do I get to the Hollywood Sign?" Since it first appeared in the Santa Monica Mountains as the Hollywoodland Sign in 1923, the sign has acted as a beacon. First, for hopeful homeowners buying plots in the Hollywoodland housing development, then eventually as a symbol of the American entertainment industry, and now—somewhat to the consternation of Angelenos—as a global tourist symbol of Los Angeles itself.

People come from all over the world to Los Angeles, and when they're here they want to see those big white letters they've dreamed about—but it hasn't always been easy to figure out how to do that.

Remember that people live in the neighborhood near the sign, so please be respectful when you're visiting.

Griffith Park itself didn't have readily available maps and wayfinding signs until about 2016, and the rise of GPS and online navigation was sending sign seekers onto narrow, winding roads that definitely weren't built to handle modern automobiles—let alone throngs of lost tourists.

Gates were locked, lawsuits were filed, and a former city councilman even lobbied Google and Garmin to change the location of the Hollywood Sign on their maps. It's still a bit of a messy situation, which is why I strongly recommend traveling on foot as much as possible when you're looking to snap your sign selfies.

Here are some of the best places to see the Hollywood Sign in and around Griffith Park depending on what kind of view you're looking for.

IF YOU WANT TO GET SOME SHOPPING DONE, TOO

Hey, who said you can't enjoy a decent view of the Hollywood Sign while also picking up a pair of jeans? The Hollywood & Highland shopping complex was L.A.'s attempt to replicate New York City's Times Square—I have some opinions about whether or not it was a *successful* attempt, but you can draw your own conclusion. It's a bit of a tourist trap, but it's pretty easy to get to without a car and there are some genuinely cool Hollywood history sites nearby, including the El Capitan Theatre, the Chinese and Egyptian Theatres, and the Roosevelt Hotel. You'll walk along the star-studded (literally) Hollywood Walk of Fame and up into the multistory outdoor shopping center, which is styled to resemble the Babylon set from the 1916 film *Intolerance*. The upper floor is angled to point you directly toward the Hollywood Sign, but you'll probably want a good zoom lens, as the sign itself is 2.4 miles away.

Location: Northwest corner of Hollywood Blvd. and Highland Ave.
Distance from Sign: 2.4 miles
How to Get There: Metro B Line Hollywood/Highland stop, DASH Hollywood, Metro bus lines 212, 222, 237, 312, and Rapid 780; paid parking in garages and on street

IF YOU WANT SOME WATER IN THE PICTURE

For what I personally consider one of the most interesting views of the Hollywood Sign, you'll want to take a nice stroll around the Hollywood Reservoir. Not only is this paved path a great place for joggers and walkers, but there are also several spots where you'll manage to get good forward-facing views of the sign with a bit of the Hollywood Reservoir in the foreground—which is not a view many people would expect to see. You can hike partway around the reservoir and shoot through a chain-link fence, but in my opinion the best views come when you're standing atop historic Mulholland Dam.

Location: Mulholland Dam
Distance from Sign: 1.3 miles
How to Get There: Hike 1

IF YOU WANT TO BEAT THE CROWDS AT LAKE HOLLYWOOD PARK

Over the past few years, Lake Hollywood Park has become a magnet for sign seekers. On clear weekend days, you can expect to see almost as many people at the unofficial viewpoint just to the south of Lake Hollywood Park as you would at the Hollywood & Highland mall.

Residents are getting frustrated with the foot and car traffic, which is why I strongly recommend hiking in instead. Following the route described in Hike 2, you won't get snarled in tourist traffic, you'll make the residents happy, *and* you'll get better views, too. First, you'll

Location: Mulholland Highway and the Innsdale Trail
Distance from Sign: 1.2 miles and 1350 feet, respectively
How to Get There: Hike 2

have some great through-the-chaparral views from the Mulholland Highway, and then on the Innsdale Trail you'll get as close to the front of the sign as you can without getting arrested.

IF YOU DON'T MIND A BEHIND-THE-SIGN VIEW

When people find out you can indeed hike up to the Hollywood Sign atop Mount Lee, few continue reading to find out that location actually gets you *behind* the sign with no way to get up close to the big white letters. Don't fret, though—any route to the top of Mount Lee is a day well spent in Griffith Park, and although the summit can get crowded on the weekends, the views can be exceptional.

There are two primary treks most people take to get to the top of Mount Lee. The route that feels most like a hike is also the shortest and steepest. Coming in from the west, the single-track trail tops out on Burbank and

Location: Summit of Mount Lee
Distance from Sign: 150 feet behind the sign
How to Get There: Hike 3 for the shorter, tougher option; Hike 7 for the longer, milder option

Cahuenga Peaks before joining Mount Lee Drive for the final short summit push. The classic route from the end of Canyon Drive is longer, but it has a gentler ascent and is on wider fire roads, meaning it's better for larger groups. Either way you choose, this is a mountain you are definitely going to want to summit at some point.

There are plenty of places where you can see the sign without having to jostle your way through throngs of tourists.

IF YOU WANT TO HIKE BUT, LIKE, JUST A LITTLE BIT

Let's say you want to get a good front-facing view of the Hollywood Sign but don't want to spend *too* much time on the trail. Maybe you're in a rush, or maybe you've got some little ones with you who don't have energy for a longer trek. No worries!

Location: Bronson Cave
Distance from Sign: About 1 mile
How to Get There: Follow directions for Hike 6

Location: West Observatory Trail
Distance from Sign: About 1.5 miles
How to Get There: Hike 9; if you head down from the observatory, you can utilize the DASH Observatory or Griffith Parkline

If you want to keep it especially short, there's a good view from the other side of the Bronson Cave with the sign behind some rugged mountain terrain. You may even recognize this scene from dozens of different films or television shows. If you're up for a bit more elevation gain and not that much more distance, there's a surprisingly excellent viewpoint on the West Observatory Trail between The Trails Café and Griffith Observatory. If you've got kiddos, both options are close to playgrounds and picnic areas, and near the West Observatory trailhead you can pick up some tasty coffee, tea, and pastries at The Trails

Café before or after your hike. Keep in mind there are some steep inclines and not a ton of shade on the West Observatory Trail, but you're not likely to find too much of a crowd at this viewpoint.

IF YOU'RE INTERESTED IN SOME SCIENCE-RELATED BONUS MATERIALS

The "official" viewing point of the Hollywood Sign has been moved to the west lawn of the Griffith Observatory, a place that the *Los Angeles Times* notes "offers a nice view, but . . . certainly not the only view or even the best view. It just happens to be the most politically expedient [one]." It's also one of the most accessible viewpoints and definitely one of the easiest to find. It keeps folks from bothering residents on the narrow streets of Hollywoodland, and for most people, the views are just fine. The crowds at the lawn can get pretty huge, especially on weekends, but you'll also have access to the free science exhibits at the Griffith Observatory and some beautiful viewpoints from the building's roof, too. Try to come here in the morning for the lightest crowds.

Location: Griffith Observatory
Distance from Sign: 1.5 miles
How to Get There: Paid parking, DASH Observatory, Griffith Parkline, or trek in on foot from Hikes 9, 10, or 14; see Hike 12 for trek to Berlin Forest from observatory

If you want a smidge more solitude, head to the north side of the observatory parking lot for the Charlie Turner Trailhead and hike up to the Berlin Forest. It's just a 0.3-mile round-trip, and there's a bit of shade in the forest, too.

IF YOU LOVE A GOOD COMMEMORATIVE VIEWPOINT

When you're looking toward the Hollywood Sign, consider that the public land you're viewing wasn't always public. In 2010, the Tiffany & Co. Foundation donated $1 million to the Trust for Public Land to secure a large tract of privately held land on Cahuenga Peak that a developer was threatening to build on. Additional generous donations from the likes of folks like Aileen Getty and Hugh Hefner and a massive public awareness campaign

Location: Tiffany & Co. Foundation Overlook on the Mount Hollywood Trail
Distance from Sign: Just over 1 mile
How to Get There: Hike 12 from the Charlie Turner Trailhead

Even with new barriers, the Hollyridge Trail (Hike 5) is still a great place to see the sign.

and fundraising effort from the City of Los Angeles secured the land, which was annexed into Griffith Park.

This official viewpoint on the Mount Hollywood Trail commemorates those efforts and also offers up an excellent view of the Hollywood Sign. Although it can get crowded here, hikers tend not to dawdle so there's usually a good turnover for the best views. Plus, you'll almost always have someone who can snap a photo for you!

IF YOU WANT A BREAK ON YOUR BIKE RIDE

If you're on a bicycle, most of the available viewpoints are a little tough to get to—but not this excellent pullout on Mount Hollywood Drive. This paved road is closed to most auto traffic and is one of the best north-south cycling routes in Griffith Park.

This viewpoint on a small western switchback of Mount Hollywood Drive provides slightly closer views than the Tiffany & Co. Foundation Overlook just above it but has

Location: Mount Hollywood Drive
Distance from Sign: About 1 mile
How to Get There: By bike on Mount Hollywood Drive; Hike 33; or hike up from the DASH Observatory stop at West Observatory Road and Mount Hollywood Drive

much lighter foot traffic and only requires a bit more navigational know-how to reach.

Other Outdoor Stuff

If you're already lacing up your hiking boots, you can skip ahead to the "Hiking Griffith Park" section. But there is so much more you can enjoy outdoors in Griffith Park—and some of these activities won't even make you break a sweat (unless you're, like, *really* chowing down those tacos).

VOLUNTEER GARDENS AND SPECIAL FORESTS

When Los Angeles was still just a growing town and far fewer people explored the trails and byways of Griffith Park, some citizens decided to leave their own personal marks here. These people took advantage of park enforcement's tendency to look the other way to set up citizen gardens, also called volunteer gardens—homegrown oases of manicured gardens inside the park. While today, trying to do something like this in the park would definitely get you in trouble—not to mention potentially cause issues with the native habitat—these small gardens remain treasured and unique spots within Griffith Park that are still cared for by volunteers.

Captain's Roost

On the western slope of Mount Hollywood, the Captain's Roost was the first of the volunteer gardens in Griffith Park—meaning

> **Reachable By:**
> Hikes 11, 12, 16, 30

this guy who people knew only as "The Captain" decided to "volunteer" his services to plant and run a garden without asking anybody if he could do so first. This man's identity remains shrouded in mystery, but by accounts of those who remember, both he and the caretakers who took over after him were not exactly friendly to others. The Captain's Roost was almost totally destroyed in the 2007 Griffith Park Fire, but volunteers have slowly been

OPPOSITE: *The rustic hand-built staircases in Amir's Garden are just one of the special touches in Griffith Park.*

The palm trees at Captain's Roost are especially photogenic at sunset.

bringing the area back to life with new drought-tolerant and native plantings. Today the roost is a small bench and narrow footpath through some lovely sage scrub and two rows of telltale palm trees, which provide an easy way to spot the area from other parts of the park.

Dante's View

One of the volunteer gardeners chased away from the Captain's Roost was a man named

Reachable By:
Hikes 11, 12, 16, 26, 30, 32, 33

Dante Orgolini, a colorful and talkative Italian polymath from Brazil. He was a journalist, actor, insurance salesman, hotel manager, and muralist—his work can be seen in the Santa Barbara Courthouse—who spoke three languages. After his marriage ended, Dante began clearing away chaparral at a viewpoint and hauling in his own plants to build a garden in 1964—again, without permission.

Reading the history of Dante's View, it becomes apparent that the man had charisma in spades. Park rangers initially tried to get him to stop building his garden, then they agreed to approve new plants he was bringing in, and eventually they just let him do his own thing and even installed water pipes leading to the garden for him. Dante went out of his way to welcome all kinds of people to Dante's View—and the kindness was returned. Dante earned a legion of volunteer caretakers who regularly celebrated the garden's founding every

FEEL LIKE GARDENING?

While many beloved volunteer gardens in Griffith Park were begun by people who started them without asking for permission, good intentions are no longer a justifiable excuse for making any kind of changes to this public park. If you do have a green thumb—or would like to learn how to get one—there's good news, though: All of these volunteer gardens still need the help of volunteers to thrive! You just need to join up with an organized group.

The Friends of Griffith Park host scheduled cleanups, plantings, and invasive plant removal at many of these locations. Visit www.friendsofgriffith park.org to see what events they have organized or click Volunteer to propose an event, or organize your own event with Recreation and Parks at www.laparks.org/info/volunteers.

October with champagne toasts (again, against the park's *official* rules) and even once with a ten-piece band who marched into the garden. His volunteers pooled money to send Dante to Italy the year before he passed away in 1978 and kept the viewpoint in great shape afterward. The next caretaker, Charlie Turner, continued pouring his heart and soul into the garden, and the trailhead he started at every day was renamed in his honor. Turner passed the baton to his assistant Tom LaBonge, who later served as a somewhat legendary city councilman from 2001 to 2015. One of LaBonge's last acts as councilman was getting Dante's View recognized as Los Angeles designated Historic-Cultural Monument #1091.

Today, despite fires and increased foot traffic, Dante's View remains a treasured landmark for locals—and a much-appreciated rest stop with shade and water for hikers and canine companions en route to Mount Hollywood.

Amir's Garden

Amir's Garden was founded by Iranian immigrant Amir Dialameh in 1971. An avid hiker (he once walked from Los Angeles to Pennsylvania on a three-month vacation), Amir was hiking near Mineral Wells after a fire and vowed to bring beauty back to the landscape. He'd immigrated to the United States in the 1960s, inspired by what he saw as a very American spirit of

Reachable By:
Hikes 22, 23, 24

The lush vegetation of Amir's Garden and the distant San Gabriel Mountains make a lovely frame for downtown Glendale.

volunteerism, and he wanted to bring that into Griffith Park. According to his own recollection on the Amir's Garden website, "I said to myself, 'This is really ugly. Somebody ought to build a garden here.' So I said, 'I'll do it' . . . and I did."

He got approval from park officials and spent the next few years essentially walking into a rugged, charred landscape to remove debris by hand. He painstakingly carved out a series of terraces and pathways, hauled up flowers and trees (and the water for them, too!), and designed and built planters, benches, tables, and chessboards—all while working a full-time job as a wine merchant. Amir eventually welcomed others who were moved by the spirit of volunteerism to help maintain this now-sprawling oasis.

Amir passed away in 2003, and longtime volunteer Kris Sabo managed his garden and kept Amir's vision blooming, adding a healthy dose of native California plants to his drought-tolerant original mix until she retired in 2018. Today, the dense greenery of Amir's Garden still stands out in the park. It remains what Amir intended it to be—"an attractive rest stop for hikers."

Berlin Forest

Hikers on the Mount Hollywood Trail heading north from the Charlie Turner Trailhead may be confused as to why a street sign showing

Reachable By:
Hikes 10, 11, 12, 16, 32, 33

Berlin, Germany, as being 5795 miles thataway is here in the midst of Griffith Park. But that's just because they've stepped into Berlin Forest.

In 1967, West Berlin, Germany, and Los Angeles became official sister cities, and nine years later visiting dignitaries brought a gift—a statue of the bear featured in the coat of arms of Berlin (the bear stands guard at the corner of Fern Dell Drive and Los Feliz Boulevard). In 1993, the mayors of several German cities visited and planted pine trees in Griffith Park to establish the Berlin Forest in celebration of this special relationship, and on the fiftieth anniversary in 2017, additional commemorative plaques and signs were installed.

When German dignitaries visit the city, they still often make a stop in Griffith Park to add another tree to the forest. A brush fire in 2018 came perilously close to this area but thankfully spared most of the Berlin Forest. Today, it's a lovely place for a picnic and an easy-to-reach, much-less-crowded spot to see the Hollywood Sign if you start off near the Griffith Observatory.

You can usually find some shade and a picnic table at the Berlin Forest.

Bird Sanctuary

In the 1920s, when Van Griffith was drawing up ambitious development plans for the park, nearby residents balked at his proposal to build

Reachable By:
Hikes 13, 30

a new zoo in Vermont Canyon, but a nice little bird sanctuary found hardly any opposition.

By the middle of that decade, the bird sanctuary was irrigated with a series of artificial streams and had become a popular stop for those looking for a quiet spot in the park. Unfortunately, drought, bark-boring beetles, invasive plantings, and fires have taken a toll. The park and volunteers have done some maintenance work in recent years and even planted new trees and cleared invasive plants, but it was definitely feeling like a forgotten corner of the park. Thankfully, in late 2019, the Friends of Griffith Park and Grown in LA kicked off a multistage habitat restoration using native plants grown at Commonwealth Nursery from Griffith Park seeds.

Today, the bird sanctuary has a small parking area, water, and restrooms. A rarely used trail meanders through the sanctuary and still provides a nice, quiet rest stop.

L.A. Aqueduct Centennial Garden

Depending on whom you ask, William Mulholland was either the savior of a thirsty Los Angeles or the villain who robbed an entire watershed of its lifeblood. Like Griffith J. Griffith, the guy was a complicated figure, but there's little doubt that Mulholland's magnum opus of engineering—the Los Angeles Aqueduct—is what allowed the pueblo to grow into the megalopolis it is today.

In 2013, the existing Mulholland Memorial Fountain was renovated to include the L.A. Aqueduct Centennial Garden, which celebrates the one-hundredth anniversary of when Mulholland opened up the floodgates, taking water from the Owens Valley and giving it to Los Angeles. The garden—which is technically outside Griffith Park on Department of Water and Power land—tells the story of the aqueduct with a short trail that mirrors its actual path and a piece of the original aqueduct that visitors can stand inside. The garden consists of drought-tolerant and California native plants, and sits near the spot where Mulholland supposedly lived in a shack when he first moved to the city.

This section of the aqueduct has become popular with portrait photographers.

Fern Canyon

Tucked away just a quick hike from Park Center is the Fern Canyon Nature Trail, which leads to a small, wild garden of California native plants

Reachable By:
Hikes 18, 30

installed by the Friends of Griffith Park as part of a fire-recovery effort.

The plantings near the Fern Canyon Amphitheater were specifically chosen because they tend to attract butterflies, and in the late winter and spring this area can truly come alive with the winged insects. Some of the plantings have labels on them, but this is a great place to come back to once you've learned a few of our local native plants—you'll see almost everything that's been planted here growing naturally throughout the rest of the park.

De Anza Native Garden

The newest special garden, the De Anza Native Garden officially opened in mid-2019 as a joint effort between Recreation and Parks, the Friends

Reachable By:
Hike 30

of Griffith Park, the National Park Service, and other groups. This small garden sits at the southeastern corner of the Wilson and Harding Golf Courses and consists entirely of plants grown from seeds gathered inside Griffith Park itself.

PARK CENTER'S RADICAL PAST

Although today a visitor to Park Center will likely just hear the sounds of the merry-go-round, tennis players, and perhaps the long-running drum circle near the film office, this area has been the center of some of Griffith Park's most radical moments. During the 1960s, Park Center was the site of numerous love-in events and unfortunately a number of violent clashes, too. From 1971 to 1975, cars were banned from Park Center on the third Sunday of every month for Sundays In the Park, where events focused on environmental awareness and a car-free lifestyle. In 1968, the city's first "Gay-In" was held near the merry-go-round. The event began with a talk by district attorney candidate (and heterosexual Los Angeles Police Department officer and socialist) Mike Hannon about police harassment of minorities and ended with Hannon joining the crowd on a gay bar crawl.

The garden lies on the Juan Bautista de Anza National Historic Trail, which marks an overland colonization route from Mexico to San Francisco that passes through Griffith Park along the Main Trail. Interpretive signs have been installed here at the garden and nearby at the Los Feliz adobe. Additional interpretive exhibits are planned along the route in the park in the future.

PICNICKING

Although you could, really, just pack some food and a blanket and bring your own picnic to a lot of different places in the park, Griffith Park does offer a number of developed picnic grounds for larger groups and—where permitted— barbecues. The larger picnic areas are some of the liveliest sections of Griffith Park, where you may see a wedding banquet setting up next to a multigenerational taco dinner (smell those homemade tortillas!), a couple lounging on hammocks, and an elaborate princess-themed birthday party.

Park Center

The Park Center picnic area is the largest of the picnic areas and often the one that's buzzing with the most activity. You'll be near tennis courts and the historic 1926 merry-go-round (open weekends and holidays from 11:00 AM to 5:00 PM), as well as within spitting distance of Shane's Inspiration playground.

Water and restrooms are close by, and vendors often set up here on the weekends and on summer evenings.

Crystal Springs
Located just east of the ranger station and visitor center and past the Pote Field baseball diamond, Crystal Springs has long been a getaway for Angelenos of all stripes. Restrooms and water are available here, as is a volleyball court. You'll also have relatively easy access to the Los Angeles River and North Atwater Park if you'd prefer to take a stroll. There are four large reservable picnic areas at Crystal Springs. Snag a reservation by calling 323-644-2050.

Old Zoo
The Old Zoo picnic area is lightly separated from Park Center by Shane's Inspiration playground but definitely has its own distinct vibe. This picnic area is

Picnickers in Griffith Park, circa 1932 (USC Digital Library, "Dick" Whittington Photography Collection)

FROM OSTRICH FARM TO PICNIC AREA

Dr. Charles Sketchley's ostrich farm in Rancho Los Feliz was more than just a place for local kids to go gawk at big birds—it was in many ways the proto L.A. Zoo, with a variety of birds and other animals, picnic grounds, trails, and even a dance floor and bar. The ostrich farm was dismantled in 1889, and the Griffith Park Zoo opened in 1912 in a place that used to be called Ostrich Farm Canyon (today the official map calls it Spring Canyon).

The zoo was small but popular, housing bears, lions, monkeys, and more. Griffith himself would walk the grounds daily and even feed some of the animals. The zoo entered its adolescence in 1913, when the city's official zoo in Eastlake Park (now called Lincoln Park) moved into the Griffith Park site. Despite new construction and funding, people were already complaining about the zoo's dilapidated condition by 1917.

The Griffith Park Master Plan of 1939 recommended abandoning it entirely, and by the 1950s it was seen as a major embarrassment for the city. After a few attempts, voters authorized a bond issue and got into a lengthy and contentious fight about where the new zoo would be located. The fight went on so long, in fact, that some people proposed to use the bond money to just build a monorail to San Diego's zoo and be done with it.

The current zoo site was approved in 1962 and opened in 1966. The Griffith Park Zoo—by now better known as the Old L.A. Zoo—was abandoned in the mid-1960s and became a magnet for vandalism and illicit activities. It reopened in 1986 as today's picnic area after a massive renovation and redevelopment effort.

a somewhat long and narrow, shaded and grassy canyon north of Lot Two that spills over into the grounds of the Old L.A. Zoo, where the Independent Shakespeare Co. performs for free every summer underneath the stars. You also have access to a number of hikes from this picnic area via the Old Zoo, Bee Rock, and Bill Eckert Trails. Water and restrooms are available.

Mineral Wells

Deeper inside the park and with more limited parking, the Mineral Wells picnic area tends to be a bit quieter than those near Park Center, although it can also get fairly crowded on weekends and holidays. This picnic area has many trees nearby and is also the trailhead for the North Trail that can take you up to Amir's Garden and deeper into the park's interior. Water and restrooms are available.

Bette Davis is one of the quieter picnic areas in the park.

Pecan Grove

Squeezed between Zoo Drive and the I-5/CA 134 interchange, the Pecan Grove picnic area is kind of an oddball among the picnic areas. It's small, not very developed, and generally passed over by folks heading to something else in the park. That all means it's often relatively calm and you probably won't have trouble finding a table. If you don't mind the noise of the freeway, it's actually very nice to take a break in this area where an actual pecan grove used to stand. A plaque marks the Juan Bautista de Anza National Historic Trail just outside the picnic area, where you're likely to see trail runners and equestrians passing by on the Main Trail.

Bette Davis

The Bette Davis picnic area is north of the Los Angeles River, so it feels like it's not a part of Griffith Park although technically it is. This large and expansive picnic area may just be the best-kept secret among picnickers—it has a lot of shade and restrooms, and provides some really lovely views of the mountainous terrain on Griffith's north end. You're also near the Los Angeles Equestrian Center, which means you'll probably also be able to wave hello to folks on horseback while you're digging into your picnic treats.

SHANE'S INSPIRATION

The largest and most active playground in Griffith Park is one of the world's first fully inclusive play areas. This beloved play area got its start with Shane Alexander Williams in 1997. Born with spinal muscular dystrophy, he passed away, sadly, just two weeks after he came into the world. His parents, Catherine Curry-Williams and Scott Williams, realized that had their son survived, there would not have been any outdoor playground in the western United States he could use with other children. With their friend Tiffany Harris, they founded the nonprofit Shane's Inspiration in 1998 with the mission of building a universally accessible playground where all children could play side by side.

The Shane's Inspiration playground in Griffith Park was opened in 2000, and since then the organization has opened over sixty playgrounds throughout the United States and around the world. The Shane's Inspiration playground in Griffith Park went through a renovation in 2019. To donate or learn how to create a Shane's Inspiration playground where you live, visit https://shanesinspiration.org.

Shane's Inspiration is teeming with fun activities and play areas for kids.

ATHLETICS

Griffith Park is home to a wide range of options for athletic activities. Keeping in spirit with the founding of the park, many if not all of these activities are either free or low-cost.

Swimming

The Griffith Park swimming pool, affectionately known as "The Plunge," is situated in the southeast corner of the park. Located in a beautiful circa-1927 building, the Plunge ties into a long history of swimming in the region. Before much of the infrastructure in Griffith Park was built, many local youths learned to swim in the Los Angeles River nearby.

In the past, the Plunge offered a variety of programs, from safety to basic swimming and even canoeing lessons. Today, the pool operates during summer months, offering Angelenos relief from the heat at very low prices as well as lifeguard training, swim lessons for youth and adults, and team sports—no more canoes, though.

The Griffith Park pool is located at 3401 Riverside Drive. Call 323-644-6878 or visit www.griffithpark.lacitypools.com for more info.

Tennis

Griffith Park has three tennis complexes—at Vermont Canyon, at the Griffith Park Recreation Center near the Plunge (called the Riverside Courts), and at Park Center. The courts at Park Center are first come, first served and may be closed on Wednesdays for cleaning. Players are expected to play one set at a time or volley for an hour and then let others take the court. Group permits are available and can be obtained by calling Park Services at 323-644-3536.

The Vermont Canyon and Riverside courts are reservable by the hour for a fee. Reserve at the Vermont Canyon courts by calling 323-664-3521 and the Recreation Center by calling 323-661-5318.

Playgrounds

Playgrounds abound in the more developed sections of the park, and over the past few years they seem to have been increasing both in number and in quality. New and renovated playgrounds have popped up in Brush Canyon near the Bronson Cave and across from the Greek Theatre, as well as near The Trails Café in Western Canyon. Shane's Inspiration in Park Center is the largest and is a landmark in its own right.

Golf

Golf in Griffith Park has a history that actually predates the park itself—the first golf course was supposedly built during the Mexican-American War by General John Baldwin when his brother Leon owned Rancho Los Feliz. This course washed away during flooding in 1884 but was refashioned into the municipal Riverside course in 1900. A modest, rough-and-tumble dirt lot, the course still proved popular enough with Angelenos to continue expanding and improving golfing facilities inside the park.

The park initiated a tradition of naming courses for the presidents who were in office when they were opened. Thus, Griffith Park now has Wilson, Harding, and Roosevelt Golf Courses as well as the Los Feliz Golf Course.

Wilson and Harding Golf Courses

The Wilson Golf Course is the longest course in the park at more than 7000 yards from the tips. This course hosts many L.A. city championship events and has hosted the Los Angeles Open. The neighboring Harding Golf Course

Address: 4730 Crystal Springs Dr.
Golf Shop: 323-663-2555
Restaurant: 323-661-7212
Website: www.golf.lacity.org /course_wilson and www.golf .lacity.org/course_harding

Golfers in Griffith enjoy beautiful views of the Verdugo Mountains.

has narrower fairways and is considered somewhat more challenging than the Wilson course.

The Wilson and Harding Courses share amenities, including practice facilities, a golf shop, driving range, and a beautiful restaurant and lounge.

Roosevelt Golf Course

The Roosevelt Golf Course is tucked into the southern end of the park, just across from the Greek Theatre on Vermont Avenue. This walking-only nine-hole course is hilly and considered to be very challenging. The course underwent renovation in 2018–2019 to switch to irrigation with recycled water.

Address: 2650 N. Vermont Ave.
Golf Shop: 323-665-2011
Café: 323-545-0444
Website: www.golf.lacity.org /course_roosevelt and franklinsatgriffithpark.com

In 2019, the Roosevelt Café also got a significant upgrade and refresh, and is now known as Franklin's Café and Market. The Market is open from 7 AM to 7 PM every day and serves a variety of sandwiches, entrees, and provisions to stock your own picnic. A breakfast menu is available and there's a lovely outdoor patio.

Los Feliz Golf Course

Across the L.A. River but still considered part of greater Griffith Park, the Los Feliz Golf Course is easily missed unless you're really looking for it. This small nine-hole par-three course is wooded and fun for casual outings.

Address: 3207 Los Feliz Blvd.
Phone: 323-663-7758
Website: www.golf.lacity.org /course_los_feliz_3_par

The course hosts movie nights in the summer, and the neighboring Los Feliz Cafe offers food and drinks.

CAMPING

While several master plans have proposed them over the years, there are no campgrounds for the general public in Griffith Park. However, two established campgrounds for youth do an incredible job of transporting Angelenos to what feels more like a classic small-town sleepaway camp than a campground in a park in the middle of the second-largest city in the United States.

COOLIDGE'S COMEBACK

On the south flank of Beacon Hill, the Coolidge Trail was for many years the last sign of the existence of the nine-hole Coolidge Golf Course. The Coolidge was kind of the redheaded stepchild of Griffith Park's fairways. The par-three course was tucked into some unusually hilly and forested terrain, and while it was never as popular as the other courses in the park, it had a small but loyal group of players.

Low admission numbers were exacerbated when California passed Prop 13 in 1978 and the funding for the cause was slashed. The course was closed in 1981 and briefly became a training ground for LAPD mounted police before being abandoned a few years later. In the early 1990s, there were efforts to turn the course into a dog park or picnic area, but instead it sat behind a chain-link fence, its grounds vandalized and graffitied.

By 2000, the grounds saw a new lease on life as the Marty Tregnan Golf Academy, named for a passionate advocate for youth golfing and forty-year member of the Municipal Golf Association. In an article on the occasion of Tregnan's death in 1997, the *Los Angeles Times* noted that he had three missions—to keep golf affordable, to keep it available to all classes and races in the city, and to maintain public control over the public golf courses in Griffith Park.

Fully renovated and revitalized, today the Marty Tregnan Golf Academy focuses on providing golfing opportunities to younger players. The academy teaches classes for golfers ages five to seventeen and also offers family golf, open practice time, seminars, and more.

Neither of these camps is open to the public, and trespassing is prohibited in both. When the camps are not running youth programs, organized groups of fifty or more people may be able to rent out the campgrounds for private events.

Camp Hollywoodland

Camp Hollywoodland, a girls' camp, is tucked into a 55-acre area near Brush Canyon beneath the Hollywood Sign. It is operated during the summer months with weekly and weekend organized programs for girls ages six to seventeen as well as parent-child sleepovers. Camp Hollywoodland is located at 3200 Canyon Drive. For program details, email camp.hollywoodland@lacity.org, call 323-467-7193, or visit www.laparks.org/camp/camp-hollywoodland.

Griffith Park Boys' Camp

The Griffith Park Boys' Camp is nestled in a canyon just to the west of the Wilson and Harding Golf Courses and has been operating in one form or another since 1926 (it was originally the girls' camp—the first boys' camp was near Travel Town). Although smaller than Camp Hollywoodland, it's surprisingly well stocked with amenities like a rock climbing wall, an archery range, a high ropes challenge course, and a swimming pool with one of the best views in L.A. The boys' camp similarly runs weekly and weekend summer programs for boys ages seven to fourteen and is located at the end of Camp Road off Griffith Park Drive. For information about programs, email gp.boyscamp@lacity.org, call 323-664-0571, or visit www.laparks.org/camp/griffith-park-boys-camp.

EQUESTRIAN ROUTES

Equestrians have been a part of this region since the days of Rancho Los Feliz, and they remain an active and vibrant community in the park today.

Most of the park's trails are built for equestrian traffic, and whether the riders are tourists looking for a unique way to experience the park or folks who board their own horses in some of the nearby equestrian residential areas, you're almost guaranteed to see someone rambling along the Griffith Park trails on horseback at some point while you're here.

If you'd like to take a ride on horseback in the park, there are a few stables nearby that will take guests on guided tours on the park trails.

You don't have to own a horse to enjoy horseback riding in Griffith Park.

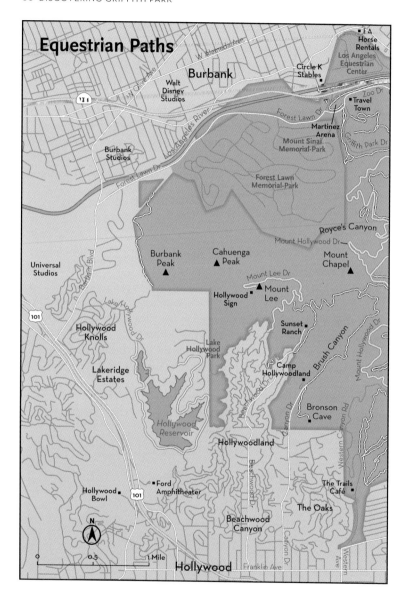

Equestrian Paths

Walt Disney Studios

Burbank

Circle K Stables

LA Horse Rentals

Los Angeles Equestrian Center

Travel Town

Forest Lawn Dr

Zoo Dr

Martinez Arena

Mount Sinai Memorial-Park

Griffith Park Dr

Burbank Studios

Forest Lawn Dr

Los Angeles River

Forest Lawn Memorial-Park

Royce's Canyon

Mount Hollywood Dr

Universal Studios

Barham Blvd

Burbank Peak ▲

Cahuenga Peak ▲

Mount Chapel ▲

Mount Lee Dr

Hollywood Sign ■ Mount Lee ▲

101

Lake Hollywood Dr

Hollywood Knolls

Lake Hollywood Park

Sunset Ranch ■

Brush Canyon

Mount Hollywood Dr

Lakeridge Estates

Camp Hollywoodland ■

Beachwood Dr

Canyon Dr

Bronson Cave ■

Western Canyon Rd

Hollywood Reservoir

Hollywoodland

Hollywood Bowl ■

101

■ Ford Amphitheater

Beachwood Dr

The Trails Café ■

The Oaks

Beachwood Canyon

Canyon Dr

Western Ave

N

0   0.5   1 Mile

Hollywood   Franklin Ave

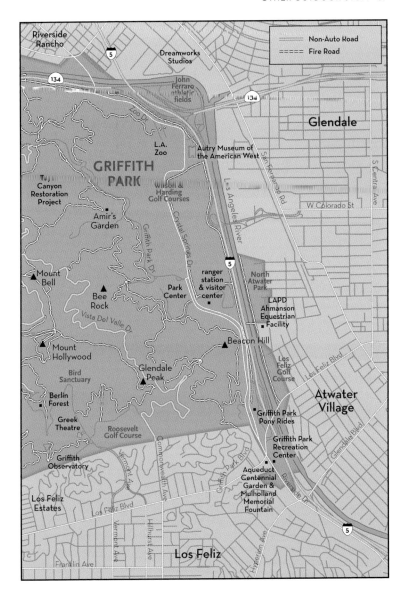

Riverside
Rancho

Dreamworks
Studios

John
Ferraro
athletic
fields

Glendale

L.A.
Zoo

Autry Museum of
the American West

**GRIFFITH
PARK**

Canyon
Restoration
Project

Wilson &
Harding
Golf Courses

W Colorado St

Amir's
Garden

Griffith Park Dr

Crystal Springs Dr

Los Angeles River

San Fernando Rd

S Central Ave

Mount
Bell

Bee
Rock

Park
Center

ranger
station
& visitor
center

North
Atwater
Park

LAPD
Ahmanson
Equestrian
Facility

Vista Del Valle Dr

Mount
Hollywood

Beacon Hill

Los
Feliz
Golf
Course

Los Feliz Blvd

Atwater
Village

Bird
Sanctuary

Glendale
Peak

Berlin
Forest

Griffith Park
Pony Rides

Greek
Theatre

Roosevelt
Golf Course

Commonwealth Ave

Griffith Park Blvd

Glendale Blvd

Griffith Park
Recreation
Center

Griffith
Observatory

Vermont Ave

Aqueduct
Centennial
Garden &
Mulholland
Memorial
Fountain

Riverside Dr

Los Feliz
Estates

Los Feliz Blvd

Hillhurst Ave

Hyperion Ave

Vermont Ave

Los Feliz

Franklin Ave

Legend:
Non-Auto Road
Fire Road

The Los Angeles Equestrian Center is open to the public for a wide variety of events.

L.A. Horse Rentals

L.A. Horse Rentals is on the north side of the park near the Los Angeles Equestrian Center. They are open seven days a week and offer timed, guided rides in the park as well as sunset rides and rides to the Hollywood Sign with an option for dinner. L.A. Horse Rentals is located at 1850 Riverside Drive in Glendale. Call 818-242-8443 or visit www.lahorserentals.com for more info.

RIDING INTO THE SUNSET?

If you take the time to walk around the neighborhoods just north of the Los Angeles River, you will often find houses with built-in horse stables and access to far-reaching equestrian paths. For many years, this area held on to a surprisingly Old West character despite its rather central location in the greater L.A. sprawl. Until as late as the 1940s, cowboys pitched tents on Rancho Providencia (the land that is now Forest Lawn Memorial-Park) and ford the L.A. River to shoot westerns at the film studios nearby, usually stopping at a saloon near today's Circle K Stable on their way home. There used to be more places to rent horses and take guided rides in Griffith Park, too—as many as seventy barns used to stand right along Riverside Drive. Now, only a handful remain. The Burbank equestrian community successfully fought off a condo developer in 2018 but seems to be under constant threats of rezoning and redevelopment.

THE DEMOCRACY OF HAM AND EGGS

In the 1920s, L.A.'s equestrian community really took to riding the trails in Griffith Park in the mornings before heading to work. As it became more popular, a sort of informal group of local mucky-mucks—including oil tycoon Edward Doheny and Hollywood movers and shakers like Cecil B. DeMille, Louis B. Mayer, and Jack and Harry Warner—formed around the ritual, and in 1924 banker Marco Hellman organized a chuckwagon breakfast at the end of the morning ride and asked a guest from Chicago to tell some stories.

Thus the foundations for the Los Angeles Breakfast Club were laid. The group enjoyed the talk so much, they all agreed to chip in $100 apiece to found an official club. President Calvin Coolidge was a guest speaker, and future president Ronald Reagan went through the still-practiced initiation ceremony for new members—which involves sitting blindfolded on a sawhorse named Ham and placing your hands in a plate of sunny-side up eggs.

The Breakfast Club meets every Wednesday morning from 7:00 AM to 9:00 am at the Friendship Auditorium and has a rotating cast of guest speakers and performers—everything from puppeteers to Zen monks, paleontologists from the La Brea Tar Pits, in-house historians from In-N-Out Burger, NASA engineers, and even an L.A. hiking guide author whose book you're reading right now. Among both the speakers and members you'll find lighthearted, charming, friendly, and knowledgeable enthusiasts of all stripes. Plus, there are sing-alongs, secret handshakes, a cryptogram, and live piano accompaniment. The meetings have a lot of in-jokes and silly rituals, but you'll catch on quickly—it's really tough to leave without a smile on your face.

Find out about new speakers and RSVP at www.labreakfastclub.com or at www.facebook.com/LABreakfastClub. Nonmembers pay $20; members pay $15 with an annual membership.

Sunset Ranch

Sunset Ranch is on the south side of the park near the top of Beachwood Canyon. Open seven days a week, they offer a variety of tours at set times (reservations are strongly recommended). They offer one- and two-hour tours as well as a two-hour evening tour and a two-hour Saturday evening tour that ends with a barbecue and live music. Sunset Ranch is at 3400 North Beachwood Drive in Los Angeles. Parking is limited, so they recommend taking a rideshare or taxi or carpooling if possible. For more info, call 323-469-5450 or visit www.sunsetranchhollywood.com.

Los Angeles Equestrian Center

The Los Angeles Equestrian Center, which is technically part of Griffith Park, does not offer rentals or trail rides at this time, but they do have boarding facilities and shopping if you already have an equine trail partner. They are also open to the public for horse shows and training and serve as a link to the larger equestrian community in the Los Angeles area. The equestrian center is located at 480 West Riverside Drive in Burbank. Call 818-840-9063 or visit www.la-equestriancenter.com for more info.

Griffith Park Pony Rides

If you're just in the mood for a quick-and-easy pony ride for the little ones, the Griffith Park Pony Rides are open year round except for Mondays and holidays. They offer a range of pony-riding experiences, from a slow and controlled "pony-go-round" to larger ponies that get up to gallopin' speed. The pony rides are located in the southeastern corner of the park at 4400 Crystal Springs Drive, Los Angeles. Call 323-664-3266 or visit www.griffithparkponyride.com for more info and pricing.

CYCLING

Los Angeles has a lot of qualities you'd expect to find in a great cycling city—generally flat terrain, a lot of paved surfaces, and an average of 284 sunny days

When the remaining stretches of the L.A. River Bike Path are complete, cyclists will be able to follow it for 32 miles to the mouth of the river at Long Beach.

Larger organized cycling groups often buzz their way through the park, especially on weekend mornings.

a year. Unfortunately, old attitudes about the dominance of cars, varying qualities of road maintenance, and heavily distracted drivers led *Bicycling* magazine to name L.A. number one on its Most Dangerous Cycling Cities list in 2018.

That said, there are certain spots in the city where riding your bike is fun and relatively safe, and Griffith Park is one of them. *While bicycles are prohibited on all dirt trails inside Griffith Park*, the park does feature a network of painted and protected bike lanes as well as a true L.A. rarity: paved roads closed to most cars! Although cyclists are still fighting for representation and respect in most places in Los Angeles, in Griffith Park there are options for leisurely rides on beach cruisers and challenging, steep slopes for more athletically focused cyclists.

Please note that *cyclists are also required to dismount and walk their bikes when using any of the tunnels in the park*. These tunnels are shared by equestrians and walkers, and are often dark and narrow.

Protected Bike Paths

There is a protected bike path that runs 7.4 miles along the west bank of the Los Angeles River from the Riverside-Victory Bridge all the way to Elysian Park. South of Griffith Park, the bike path runs through the neighborhood of Frogtown, where riders can exit at a number of parks and a growing number of local businesses, including Spoke Bicycle Cafe, Frogtown Brewery, and the Friends of the L.A. River's Frog Spot at Lewis MacAdams Riverfront Park, where free events and educational programming are held during the warmer months.

At the time of writing, there are three access points to the L.A. River Bike Path from Griffith Park. One lies in the north end of the park, near the Riverside-Victory Bridge over the 134. Riders can access the bike path heading east—the path to the west is under construction. The second is near the Zoo Drive exit off the 5, near the John Ferraro athletic fields. Both the Riverside-Victory Bridge and Zoo Drive entrances are scheduled to be reopened right around the time this book is published.

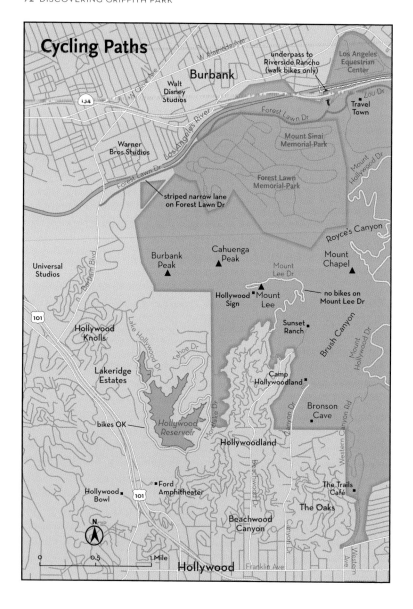

Cycling Paths

W Alameda Ave

W Olive Ave

134

Burbank

Walt Disney Studios

underpass to Riverside Rancho (walk bikes only)

Los Angeles Equestrian Center

Zou Dr

Travel Town

Warner Bros Studios

Los Angeles River

Forest Lawn Dr

Forest Lawn Dr

Mount Sinai Memorial Park

Forest Lawn Memorial-Park

Mount Hollywood Dr

striped narrow lane on Forest Lawn Dr

Royce's Canyon

Universal Studios

Barham Blvd

Burbank Peak ▲

Cahuenga Peak ▲

Mount Lee Dr

Mount Chapel ▲

Hollywood Sign ▪ Mount Lee ▲

no bikes on Mount Lee Dr

101

Hollywood Knolls

Lake Hollywood Dr

Tahoe Dr

Sunset Ranch ▪

Brush Canyon

Mount Hollywood Dr

Lakeridge Estates

Camp Hollywoodland ▪

bikes OK

Hollywood Reservoir

Mount Lake Dr

Bronson Cave

Western Canyon Rd

Hollywoodland

Hollywood Bowl ▪

101

▪ Ford Amphitheater

Beachwood Dr

The Trails Café ▪

The Oaks

N

Beachwood Canyon

Canyon Dr

0   0.5   1 Mile

Hollywood

Franklin Ave

Western Ave

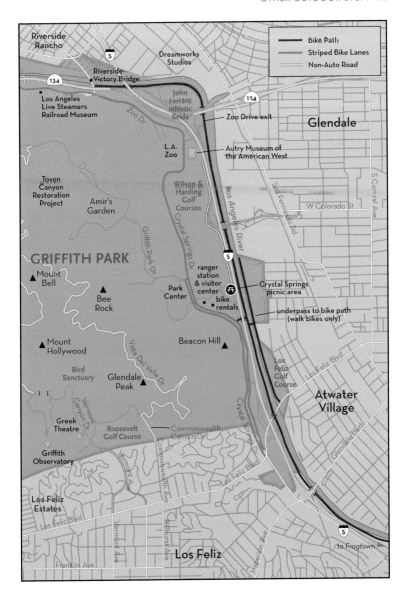

Riverside
Rancho

5

Dreamworks
Studios

Riverside-
Victory Bridge

134

Zoo Dr

John
Ferraro
athletic
fields

134

Zoo Drive exit

Los Angeles
Live Steamers
Railroad Museum

L.A.
Zoo

Autry Museum of
the American West

Glendale

Toyon
Canyon
Restoration
Project

Amir's
Garden

Wilson &
Harding
Golf
Courses

Los Angeles River

S Central Ave

S Fernando Rd

W Colorado St

Griffith Park Dr

Crystal Springs Dr

GRIFFITH PARK

Mount
Bell

Bee
Rock

5

ranger
station
& visitor
center

Park
Center

bike
rentals

Crystal Springs
picnic area

underpass to bike path
(walk bikes only)

Mount
Hollywood

Vista Del Valle Dr

Beacon Hill

Los
Feliz
Golf
Course

Los Feliz Blvd

**Atwater
Village**

Bird
Sanctuary

Glendale
Peak

Vermont Canyon Dr

Greek
Theatre

Roosevelt
Golf Course

Commonwealth
Canyon Dr

Crystal Springs Dr

Glendale Blvd

Griffith
Observatory

Commonwealth Ave

Vermont Ave

Los Feliz Blvd

Los Feliz
Estates

Los Feliz Blvd

Hillhurst Ave

Hyperion Ave

5

to Frogtown

Franklin Ave

Vermont Ave

Los Feliz

Bike Path

Striped Bike Lanes

Non-Auto Road

The last access point is through a mildly creepy cement tunnel beneath the 5 freeway at the south end of the Crystal Springs picnic area. Prominent signs say "No Bicycles Allowed," but rangers have told me you can walk your bike through the tunnel. The equestrians who also use the tunnel will be very appreciative. Unfortunately, the nearby striped bike lane on Crystal Springs Drive does not connect to this underpass, so you'll have to walk your bike along the Main Trail to the pavement.

A bridge is expected to be completed soon that will connect the L.A. River Bike Path with North Atwater Park and bike infrastructure on the east side of the L.A. River in the Atwater neighborhood on the other side of this tunnel. The bridge will have dedicated areas for pedestrians, cyclists, and equestrians.

Plans are also underway to extend the L.A. River Bike Path through downtown Los Angeles to another section that begins in the city of Vernon, which will create a 32-mile-long protected bike path from the north side of Griffith Park to the Pacific Ocean at Long Beach—part of a greater plan to revitalize and restore the Los Angeles River. It's an incredibly exciting project that includes new parks and a new respect and appreciation for the Los Angeles River, but it also will likely take many, many years to complete.

Please note that the L.A. River Bike Path may be closed during rainy days for safety. Don't be lulled into a sense of security when you see the trickle of the river during the summer months—that ribbon of water can still cause some serious damage during the wet season.

Bike Lanes

A striped, separated bike lane runs uninterrupted from the Warner Bros. Studios lot in Burbank all the way to Los Feliz Boulevard in the southeast corner of Griffith Park. In most places along that route, cars aren't allowed to park, so you don't have to worry about getting doored! (You do still need to watch out for speeding cars and places where the lane narrows, though.)

The bike lanes connect with many highlights in the park, including Travel Town, the Los Angeles Live Steamers Railroad Museum, the L.A. Zoo, the Autry Museum of the American West, the Wilson and Harding Golf Courses, Shane's Inspiration, the merry-go-round, the ranger station and visitor center, pony and train rides, and several picnic areas and playgrounds as well. Sharrow lanes extend the bike network north along Riverside Drive to Riverside Rancho and the Bette Davis picnic area and Los Angeles Equestrian Center.

Mount Hollywood and Vista Del Valle Drive inside the park serve as rare, car-free roads for cyclists.

Mostly Car-Free Roads

Cyclists looking for some more elevation gain and challenging rides can enjoy riding on nearly any paved road in the park, but the real gems here are Mount Hollywood Drive and Vista Del Valle Drive, two winding mountain roads snaking through the center of Griffith Park that have been closed to automobile through-traffic since 1991 (save for the occasional maintenance vehicle, car commercial, or film shoot).

The two roads can sometimes be rough, but careful, attentive cyclists shouldn't have trouble navigating them. Remember that equestrians sometimes use these roads, too!

Bike Rentals

Didn't bring your own bike to the park? Or just got the urge to be on two wheels after you arrived? From Memorial Day through Labor Day, you can rent several types of bikes—including low-rider bikes and surrey carriages—from an outpost of local bike shop Spokes 'N Stuff located next to the ranger station and visitor center. The rental shop is open from 2:00 PM to sunset during the week and 10:30 AM to sunset on weekends, and is closed when it is raining. Call 323-662-6573 or visit www.spokes-n-stuff.com for more info.

Museums and Cultural Attractions

Los Angeles has more museums per capita than any other city in the world, and some truly world-class institutions make their home inside the park. You probably know about—or at least have seen—the Griffith Observatory and Los Angeles Zoo, but there are also some quirkier destinations that are well worth your time.

GRIFFITH OBSERVATORY

A beautiful Depression-era monument to the stars

Address: 2800 East Observatory Rd., Los Angeles
Phone: 213-473-0800
Website: www.griffithobservatory.org
Hours: Noon to 10:00 PM weekdays, 10:00 AM to 10:00 PM weekends, closed Mondays and some holidays
Admission: Free, but admission required for planetarium shows
Accessible By: DASH Observatory shuttle, Griffith Parkline (weekends), car, foot

This world-famous Works Progress Administration (WPA) building was one of the few improvements to the park personally envisioned and started by Griffith J. Griffith. Recently renovated, this iconic structure houses one of the first planetariums in the United States, stunning murals and sculptures, the largest astronomically accurate image ever created, and a science museum that has not charged admission since its completion in 1935. It's also a fantastic spot for city views and nighttime star parties.

OPPOSITE: *Famous from appearances in films and television and an architectural gem in its own right, the Griffith Observatory is a true L.A. icon.*

GETTING THERE

PUBLIC TRANSIT The Los Angeles Department of Transportation (LADOT) operates the DASH Observatory shuttle Monday through Friday from noon to 10:00 PM and on weekends from 10:00 AM to 10:00 PM. It is by far the most convenient way to get to the observatory. The DASH shuttle stops at the Greek Theatre, at several stops in the Los Feliz neighborhood, and at the Vermont/Sunset subway station. The Griffith Parkline also stops at the observatory. Visit www.ladottransit.com for fares and schedules.

DRIVING From Los Feliz Boulevard, head north on Fern Dell Drive, Vermont Avenue, or Hillhurst Avenue. Parking near the observatory is paid by the hour and has no time limit during the operating hours of the observatory. Paid parking is via credit card only. Parking before the observatory is open is free. You may also park for free in the Greek Theatre parking lot (when the theater has no events scheduled) or north of The Trails Café (lot closes at sunset).

BY FOOT If you park near The Trails Café or are coming into the park from Fern Dell, you can reach the observatory via the Observatory Trails (Hike 9) or on the Western Canyon to Berlin Forest Loop (Hike 10). From the Greek Theatre parking lot, you can head south past the theater and use the Boy Scout Trail (Hike 14). A pedestrian sidewalk runs from the Greek Theatre parking lot to the observatory.

After the Hollywood Sign, the Griffith Observatory may very well be the most recognizable structure in Griffith Park. Perfectly situated on a ledge overlooking the Los Feliz neighborhood and artfully lit at night following a massive renovation in 2006, the observatory allegedly began after Griffith J. Griffith visited the observatories on Mount Wilson in the San Gabriel Mountains with then–county supervisor John Anson Ford. According to Ford's account, Griffith gazed through the telescope and had a precursor to Carl Sagan's famous "pale blue dot" idea, exclaiming, "If all mankind could look through that telescope, it would revolutionize the world!"

The observatory rooftop has some of the best views in the park.

At the time, most observatories were only accessible to professional astronomers and scientists. Much in the same way Griffith wanted to make sure all people had access to parks—and perhaps taking a bit of inspiration from the nearby Lowe Astronomical Observatory above Echo Mountain in Altadena—he wanted to bring the heavens down to the common Angeleno.

In 1912, Griffith pledged $100,000 to the construction of a public observatory and hall of science atop Mount Hollywood in Griffith Park. He hoped to have things ready to go in a few years, but problems with the chosen site, political infighting, and a lingering hesitancy to accept a gift from a guy who shot his wife in the face stalled construction until 1933—well after Griffith's death in 1919.

The Great Depression made construction and labor relatively cheap and the New Deal–era emphasis on employing artisans on projects gave the completed building a beautiful, monumental flair. The Griffith Park Trust commissioned polymath Hugo Ballin to create the stunning murals depicting the history of stargazing and science in the rotunda, and one of the six artists who designed the *Astronomers Monument* on the observatory's front lawn in 1934 sculpted the original Oscar statue for just $500 back in 1929.

During its opening week in 1935, 17,739 excited people packed the observatory and what was then only the third planetarium in the United States. Today, more people have viewed the heavens through the Griffith Observatory's Zeiss 12-inch refracting telescope than any other telescope on Earth, and the observatory is the most visited public observatory in the world. I think we can chalk that one under the "win" column for the Colonel, don't you?

DON'T MISS

The observatory holds volunteer-run public star parties once a month from 2:00 PM to 9:45 PM. Check the website for dates and conditions. *The Big Picture* is the largest astronomical image on Earth—it measures 150 feet long and 40 feet tall and contains 700,000 stars and a million galaxies. The nearby statue of Einstein shows you that all those stars are visible in the space of about one inch on a human finger held up against the night sky. Also, for my money, the presenting staff of the Samuel Oschin Planetarium is the most enthusiastic and engaged in the galaxy.

AUTRY MUSEUM OF THE AMERICAN WEST

An interesting and innovative museum about the West featuring stories too often left untold

Address: 4700 Western Heritage Way, Los Angeles
Phone: 323-667-2000
Website: https://theautry.org
Hours: Tuesday–Friday 10:00 AM to 4:00 PM, weekends 10:00 AM to 5:00 PM, closed Mondays (special events and performances may have longer hours)
Admission: Paid admission but free on the second Tuesday of every month and on New Year's Day; Los Angeles Public Library cardholders 18 and over may reserve a limited number of free passes per year (www.lapl.org/explorela)
Accessible By: Griffith Parkline (weekends), bus, car, foot

This museum goes far beyond popular portrayals of the region to include strong voices traditionally excluded from stories of the West. There are the sweeping landscape art and cowboy frontier stories you'd expect but also boundary-pushing installations, lectures, and theater from Native American artists, Chicano and Latinx histories, and multimedia exhibits that question what it means to be an Angeleno, a Californian, and a Westerner.

GETTING THERE

PUBLIC TRANSIT   The Griffith Parkline and Metro bus 96 stop here.
DRIVING   From the 134 westbound, exit at Zoo Drive and take a left on Western Heritage Way.
BY FOOT   The museum is just off the Main Trail, but in this corner of the park the trail is used primarily by runners and equestrians. However, if you are hiking on the Rattlesnake and Skyline Loop (Hike 27), you can hike east on the Main Trail to visit the museum halfway through your trek.

The Autry Museum of the American West (or simply "the Autry") was cofounded by the legendary Singing Cowboy himself as the Gene Autry Western Heritage Museum in 1988. Building from Autry's personal collection of artifacts and memorabilia, the museum in its early days often mixed real-life artifacts with fictionalized memorabilia from Western films and television series—Annie Oakley's gold-plated guns could be found just a few rooms over from bedazzled, sequined cowboy costumes from Hollywood musicals.

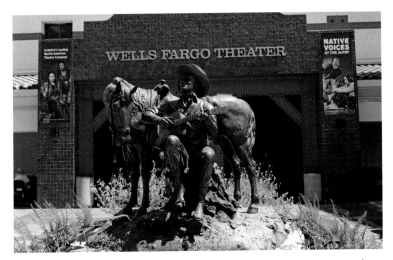

"The Autry" brings the diverse and complex stories of the West's past, present, and future to life year-round.

But since its founding, the Autry has reexamined its purpose and role as a museum in Los Angeles with exceptional results. In 1995, the Native Voices theater program was founded—the only equity theater that focuses on producing new works by Native American, Alaska Native, and First Nations playwrights. In 2002, the museum merged with Colorado's Women of the West Museum and became a research and educational landmark for scholars of the region (a new research facility is slated to open in Burbank in 2020).

Major renovations and a merger with the Southwest Museum of the American Indian (L.A.'s first museum) broadened the scope even further with installations like *Human Nature*, which investigates modern-day California issues using the histories of its indigenous peoples, and *La Raza*, a stunning collection of photographs from the groundbreaking Los Angeles newspaper at the center of the Chicano rights movement.

The Autry also hosts lectures, guided tours, outdoor movies and screenings of classic and rarely seen Westerns, night markets, and an annual Western art show and American Indian Arts Marketplace. And don't worry—there are still singing cowboys (and gals) who perform the third Sunday of every month, and they know how to put on a show!

DON'T MISS

The stunning, 7000-square-foot outdoor ethnobotanical garden highlights over sixty California native plant species and their traditional and modern uses—it's a great way to recognize plants you see on hikes, get inspiration for your own garden, or just take a quick breather in a peaceful outdoor space between exhibits. Through 2024, the museum's community-driven *Investigating Griffith Park* exhibit will be the first to focus on the many fascinating stories the park has to offer . . . which will no doubt be of interest to readers of *this* book. Also, the Crossroads West Cafe is probably the healthiest food you can get this far from The Trails Café.

LOS ANGELES ZOO AND BOTANICAL GARDENS

A 133-acre zoo and botanical garden, home to more than 270 different species, including 58 endangered species

Address: 5333 Zoo Dr., Los Angeles
Phone: 323-644-4200
Website: www.lazoo.org
Hours: 10:00 AM to 5:00 PM daily, closed December 25
Admission: Paid admission; Los Angeles Public Library cardholders 18 and over may reserve a limited number of free passes per year (www.lapl.org/explorela)
Accessible By: Griffith Parkline (weekends), bus, car, foot

The L.A. Zoo is a family-friendly destination for animal lovers that offers many opportunities to see species both up close and in excellent approximations of their natural habitats. It is also a leader in worldwide conservation and species rehabilitation.

GETTING THERE

PUBLIC TRANSIT The Griffith Parkline and Metro bus 96 stop here.
DRIVING From the 5 northbound, take the exit for CA 134 eastbound and keep right to exit on Zoo Drive. Stay straight at the intersection with Western Heritage Way. There is a large parking lot in front of the L.A. Zoo. Parking is free, but preferential parking (read: closer to the entrance) can be had for a fee.
BY FOOT The zoo can be reached on the Main Trail, but you may also be able to get a glimpse of some of the aviaries while hiking on the Oak Canyon Loop (Hike 28). Even if you can't see the chimpanzees, you'll almost *definitely* be able to hear them.

Zoos have a long history in Griffith Park. In fact, one of the first attractions in this area was an ostrich farm that used to be near the merry-go-round. The old Griffith Park Zoo followed nearby in 1912, but almost as soon as it was built, it was obsolete and kind of an embarrassment to the city (see Hike 20).

The present-day site was approved in 1962, and it opened in December of 1966. This new zoo has been a tremendous improvement over the Old L.A. Zoo, leading both in conservation efforts as well as modernized facilities for its animals. In the 1980s, the L.A. Zoo was a major partner in the California Condor Recovery Program. By that time, the enormous birds had been reduced to just 22 individuals in the wild—mostly due to poisoning from lead ammunition. Today, there are over 400 in the world, with half living in the wild.

Extensive renovations in the 1990s and 2000s significantly updated many animal enclosures—the *Elephants of Asia* exhibit alone now commands 3.8 acres of space in the zoo—and an ambitious vision plan aims to continue those trends in the future with a spotlight on sustainability, animal rehabilitation, and native California species.

The L.A. Zoo is one of the most popular attractions inside Griffith Park. (Jamie Pham, Greater Los Angeles Zoo Association)

DON'T MISS

The L.A. Zoo offers up a number of up close-and-personal and behind-the-scenes experiences for an additional fee with zoo admission or membership, including chances to feed flamingos and giraffes, spend time working with the zoo's animal care staff, and more. The zoo also has regular programs throughout the week as well as special programs depending on the season, weather, and cooperation of the animal participants, of course. A full schedule can be found at www.lazoo.org/visit/showsandactivities or by calling the zoo. I strongly recommend the long-running "World of Birds" show (daily Wednesday through Monday at noon and 2:30 PM), which is a fantastic exhibition of the natural behaviors of macaws, vultures, cranes, hawks, and—most notably—Hope, the world's first California condor to participate in a free-flight bird show.

Railfans owe it to themselves to spend some time at Travel Town.

TRAVEL TOWN

One of the largest and most distinctive transportation museums in the country

Address: 5200 Zoo Dr., Los Angeles
Phone: 323-662-5874
Website: www.traveltown.org
Hours: 10:00 AM to 4:00 PM weekdays, 10:00 AM to 5:00 pm winter weekends (Nov.–Feb.) and 10:00 AM to 6:00 pm summer weekends (Mar.–Oct.)
Admission: Free, but miniature train rides require a fee
Accessible By: Griffith Parkline (weekends), car, foot

Originally conceived as a "petting zoo" for trains, Travel Town has since been on a strange and winding track. Although trains are definitely the focus, transportation of all kinds is treasured and honored here. Volunteers can participate in model train clubs or even work on the restoration of historic locomotives, and space inside some of the train cars can be rented out for birthday parties and other celebrations. This is a must-visit for train aficionados of all ages. Plus, it's free!

GETTING THERE
PUBLIC TRANSIT The Griffith Parkline stops here.
DRIVING From the 134, take the Forest Lawn exit and enter Griffith Park via Zoo Drive. Travel Town is straight ahead.
BY FOOT Travel Town is at the end of the Cub to Caboose route (Hike 32).

As far as museums go, Travel Town is a bit of a throwback to the very old-school definition of the word—which was basically "Hey, here's a bunch of cool stuff I put together. Wanna see?" In 1947, the city's superintendent of Recreation and Parks, William Frederickson Jr., noticed the government was disposing of a lot of outdated war equipment like planes, and he thought kids would have a fun time crawling on them. He convinced the board at the time to pony up a couple hundred dollars for some planes, but by the time they got the paperwork filed, the planes had gone off somewhere else.

The idea persisted, though, and when Frederickson's employee Charley Atkins took over the project, he decided to go for trains instead. In the early

LAND OF MANY USES

The land in Griffith Park has a long history of being used for many things, but the federal government has had some interesting history in the region where Travel Town now sits. The first modern, developed use of this land was for the municipal boys' camp—a sleepaway campground and outdoor center for young boys on the banks of the Los Angeles River. The camp was then transferred to the State Emergency Relief Administration for transient youth, then to the storied Civilian Conservation Corps from 1938 to 1940 as one of three CCC camps in Griffith Park for crews building trails, roads, and other infrastructure.

After the bombing of Pearl Harbor, the camp was hastily turned into a detention center for Japanese American "enemy aliens." Oral histories estimate that as many as 550 Japanese Americans were held in Griffith Park between 1941 and 1942 before being sent to internment camps in other parts of the country. (For those interested in this history, Manzanar National Historic Site north of Lone Pine is a powerful place to visit.) After the war, the site was used to process prisoners of war and later served as a photographic and camouflage laboratory before being dismantled and returned to the park in 1947.

The only trace of history on the site is the 1993 replica statue of "Iron Mike," officially called *Spirit of the CCC*. The original statue was crafted for a visit by President Franklin D. Roosevelt and his wife, Eleanor, in 1935 but vanished under mysterious circumstances.

1950s, most train companies were retiring obsolete steam engines, and Atkins and his train-loving buddies wanted to preserve these historic machines. Train companies were enthusiastic and so was the Department of Recreation and Parks, and some of the first trains donated were locomotives that had helped build the Port of Los Angeles (Trains #31 and #32, still on display today).

Travel Town was a hit when it opened in 1952—and was somewhat a victim of its own success. The collection grew quickly and without a real sense of direction, which muddled any semblance of coherent messaging about the museum. Also, the well-intentioned openness of the museum—kids could literally crawl all over these machines, and initially nothing was guarded at night—led to vandalism and an unfortunate loss of many historic artifacts.

The museum later went through some shuffling and reorganization, and is now hoping to hone its mission and focus as well as to step up its historic preservation and restoration efforts.

DON'T MISS

Free docent tours are held the second Saturday of every month from 11:00 AM to 3:00 PM and will greatly increase your enjoyment of the displays of Travel Town. This is the only way you can enter some of the museum's prized possessions, like the 1937 Union Pacific dormitory and club car known as the Little Nugget. Its club interior was designed to stand out from the sleek, streamlined designs of the era—so its designer, American artist Walt Kuhn, went with a somewhat gaudy Old West saloon look instead. In 1990, the Little Nugget was designated Los Angeles Historic-Cultural Monument #474. There's also a fire-engine-red four-motor electric locomotive that was used to help build the first subway tunnels in downtown Los Angeles at the turn of the century *and* to help rebuild San Francisco after the 1906 earthquake.

LOS ANGELES LIVE STEAMERS RAILROAD MUSEUM

A volunteer-run museum and demonstration ground for scale railroads

Address: 5202 Zoo Dr., Los Angeles
Phone: 323-661-8958
Website: www.lalsrm.org
Hours: Sundays only, 11:00 AM to 3:00 PM; larger grounds open on third Sunday of the month
Admission: Free; donations accepted; admission for train rides (riders must be at least 34 inches tall and weigh less than 350 pounds; children under 18 must be accompanied by an adult)
Accessible By: Griffith Parkline (weekends), car, foot

The Los Angeles Live Steamers Railroad Museum is a bargain-priced delight for kids and train enthusiasts of all ages. The museum features steam, diesel, and electric locomotives, and you're likely to see volunteer staff tending to machines or tweaking the run of the track on your visit, too. Get here early to avoid lines.

The scale train rides at Live Steamers are legitimately fun and surprisingly long.

GETTING THERE

PUBLIC TRANSIT The Griffith Parkline stops here.

DRIVING From the 134, exit at Forest Lawn Drive and turn left to enter Griffith Park via Zoo Drive. At Travel Town, keep left to continue on Zoo Drive. There is a small dirt lot just to the east of Los Angeles Live Steamers Railroad Museum as well as street parking on Zoo Drive.

BY FOOT The barn is reachable via the Rattlesnake and Main Trails on the north side of the park. Hike 27 is a nice loop that can be done before or after your visit, and you could also head down the Rattlesnake Trail from the route to Royce's Canyon (Hike 29).

Founded in 1956 by a growing group of railroad enthusiasts, the Los Angeles Live Steamers found an ally in Charley Atkins (he of neighboring Travel Town). Atkins helped the group get a conditional permit for operation in Griffith Park and donated a passenger car that later became the group's on-site meeting house.

The group has relied on volunteer efforts and donations from friends to create what has become a truly charming and sprawling little railway system.

The museum has all kinds of railroad artifacts and paraphernalia. During the Halloween season, members periodically construct an elaborate family-friendly haunted house along the entire track. It's called the Ghost Train and is definitely worth the increased price and sometimes long lines. If you're lucky, you may also be able to visit a nearby haunted area called Boney Island as well.

On most Sundays, visitors can ride the trains and watch volunteers at work, but on the third Sunday of every month, the larger grounds are open. Then, you can get a closer look at interactive, scale model engines and an operational stationary steam plant that runs seven different vintage engines, as well as have access to the Carolwood Barn (see next entry).

DON'T MISS
The ride on the scale model trains is surprisingly long and a delight from beginning to end. The train operates on a track that's about a mile long on 13 acres, and the route snakes around miniature buildings, through tunnels, and across bridges. The trains travel outside the main grounds and past a nearby picnic area as well, giving you plenty of time to wave to little trainspotters along the way.

WALT DISNEY'S CAROLWOOD BARN

Often called the "Birthplace of Imagineering"

Address: 5202 Zoo Dr., Los Angeles
Phone: 818-934-0173
Website: www.carolwood.com
Hours: 11:00 AM to 3:00 PM, the third Sunday of every month
Admission: Free, but donations accepted
Accessible By: Griffith Parkline (weekends), car, foot

This nondescript barn used to sit on Walt Disney's property in the Holmby Hills neighborhood of Los Angeles. Walt spent countless hours here tinkering with a scale railway and often brainstorming ideas for his empire with early Disney artists, musicians, and engineers. The barn is stuffed to the brim with Disney history, artifacts, and paraphernalia, and is staffed by friendly and knowledgeable docents from the Carolwood Society.

GETTING THERE

PUBLIC TRANSIT The Griffith Parkline stops here.

DRIVING From the 134, exit at Forest Lawn Drive and turn left to enter Griffith Park via Zoo Drive. At Travel Town, keep left to continue on Zoo Drive. There is a small dirt lot just to the east of Los Angeles Live Steamers Railroad Museum as well as street parking on Zoo Drive.

BY FOOT The barn is reachable via the Rattlesnake and Main Trails on the north side of the park. Hike 27 is a nice loop that can be done before or after your visit, and you could also head down the Rattlesnake Trail from the route to Royce's Canyon (Hike 29).

I t's not revolutionary to say that Walt Disney has a somewhat legendary status in American culture, but it may be surprising to learn that he also has a strong connection to Griffith Park. There are many stories about Walt visiting Griffith Park to get inspired by this or that aspect for an upcoming film or project. Disney himself recollected taking his children to ride the Griffith Park merry-go-round many times, which some have said may have inspired him to work on a theme park. There are apocryphal stories of him strolling the canyon at Fern Dell to think of design ideas for folks waiting in line at the future Disneyland, but the Carolwood Barn is an undeniable connection to the man who initially wanted to build that happiest of places just a few miles to the west.

By the 1940s, Disney Studios had released enough films and animated reels to make their mark, and like many rich creative types, Walt wanted to do something fun with his money—so after being inspired by a visit to a railroad fair in Chicago in 1948, he decided to build a scale railway for his home on Carolwood Drive. No minor hobby, the Carolwood Pacific Railroad (as Walt called it) ran for 2615 feet and included a 46-foot-long trestle bridge and a 90-foot-long tunnel under his wife Lillian's flower bed. It was completed in 1950.

To design this railway, Walt took a barn built for the Disney film *So Dear to My Heart* and moved it to the Carolwood property as his private tinkering getaway space. The barn is said to have been modeled on one that the Disney family owned in Marceline, Missouri, from 1906 to 1910. Walt hand made much of the interior, including a washbasin where he shaved every morning before getting to work (his shaving brush is still on display).

Walt would often invite other early Disney Studios employees over to tinker and brainstorm ideas for films and eventually designs for Disneyland and several rides. Walt died in 1966, and Lillian donated the track of the Carolwood Pacific to Los Angeles Live Steamers the following year.

After Lillian Disney died in 1997, the Carolwood property was sold. Walt's daughter Diane Disney Miller worked with the Carolwood Society to dismantle and preserve the Carolwood Barn. In 1999, it was given on loan to Los Angeles Live Steamers and opened to the public that year.

Today this museum inside another museum is a must-visit for Disney fanatics of all ages (so be sure to get there early!). Just outside the barn, the Carolwood Foundation is working on restoring an original passenger car from the Disneyland Railroad.

DON'T MISS

There's a *lot* to see in this little barn, but definitely check out a small shelf on the upper eastern wall, where you can see a 1951 rendering of the original location of Disneyland Park—which would have been just a stone's throw from where you're standing. Today, the lot that was to be Disneyland is home to ABC Television and the Walt Disney Animation Studios.

Disney's beloved Carolwood Barn now stands just a short distance away from the headquarters of the global media company he founded.

Hiking in Griffith Park

Whether you're in the mood for a full-day trek or a calming walk in the woods, Griffith Park has—depending on whom you ask—fifty-something or seventy-something miles of trails. I'll get to that discrepancy in just a minute . . . and yes, I'll give you detailed directions to the Hollywood Sign, too—and help prevent you from having your car ticketed or towed (or from getting yelled at by an angry resident).

WHAT YOU'LL NEED

Griffith Park is a city park, so you won't need to get all decked out in your finest backpacking gear here, but it is also a surprisingly rugged wilderness that requires a bit more respect and preparation than a stroll around the neighborhood.

While there are certainly some easy, short trails here—and many routes that can be done with just a solid pair of grippy athletic shoes and gym clothes—know your limits, read up on the terrain of the route you're going on, and prepare accordingly. I can't tell you how many people I've seen in jeans and tennis or dress shoes wandering around the park's interior trails looking for the Hollywood Sign without food, water, or a map.

There is information on the flora and fauna earlier in the book, including some of the potentially dangerous things you may run into on the trail.

For the most part, hikers here get in trouble when they're underprepared, especially during the summer when temperatures in the afternoon can spike and shade is rare or nonexistent. If you can, start your hikes early to beat crowds and enjoy cooler temperatures.

Wear clothing that protects you from the sun and is breathable. Use sunscreen, and always bring snacks and water—I recommend at least a liter per

OPPOSITE: *The Powerline Trail (Hike 4) is one of the least-traveled trails in the park.*

person for every trail in this book. Bring more if you're a thirsty hiker, and note locations of places where you can fill up along the trail if needed.

The trails in the park can get confusing, especially in the interior. Always bring a paper map with you, whether it's this book or a map from the visitor center. Do not rely on your cell phone—coverage is spotty in many places in the park.

If you're the type of person who likes a good checklist, The Mountaineers originated the Ten Essentials, which is designed to help make sure you have what you need to prevent an emergency or to respond to one in case it occurs, and to ensure you can safely spend a night outdoors if that need arises. Some of them may seem like overkill in a park that's inside a city, but the idea here is "better safe than sorry." The Ten Essentials are:

1. Navigation
2. Headlamp
3. Sun protection
4. First aid
5. Multitool
6. Fire
7. Shelter
8. Extra food
9. Extra water
10. Extra clothes

For the purposes of exploring within the L.A. city limits, please note that it is illegal to carry a knife in plain view. Also, obviously, you don't want to start a fire in the middle of an often dry natural area like Griffith Park. These essentials are more for long hikes into wilderness areas, but certain areas of this park can prove challenging, especially to the unprepared. Use your common sense to pack and prepare for any outing.

Urban Hiking

Beyond the basic personal safety stuff of responsibly enjoying outdoor activities, it is wise to remember that Griffith Park is a large, rugged, popular city park in a huge urban environment. Although you will be out enjoying nature and in all likelihood will not experience any serious issues while you're here, it is wise to exercise a certain base level of "street smarts" along with your outdoor survival knowledge.

It is advisable to hike with a buddy whenever possible. There are also a large number of organizations that lead free group hikes inside the park, from

Hikers stop for a rest in the Berlin Forest (Hike 10).

the Sierra Club and the Griffith Park rangers to amateur groups who organize on Facebook or Meetup.

HOW TO CHOOSE A TRAIL

For each hike, the trail information is broken down to help you determine which routes are best for you. You'll see basic things like distance, elevation gain and high point, and difficulty, along with the time *an average hiker* should budget for the journey. Your time may differ depending on how fast you hike, how many photos you like to take, or whether or not you brought a book to read when you take a break. The at-a-glance chart at the end of this hike introduction gives you a great overview.

I've broken trail difficulty down into four categories: easy, moderate, challenging, and very challenging. The difficulty rating is for an average hiker—someone who gets out onto the trails regularly but may only do so on the weekends as a quick escape. If you're the type of hiker who routinely summits 14ers, you'll likely find the trails in Griffith Park interesting but not terribly challenging. These are subjective labels, but there is a bit of a system:

Easy trails are those that pretty much everyone will be able to do, including tourists in slacks and dress shoes. Most are relatively flat, although they may have some short sections of incline. Don't be lulled into total complacency, though—as noted in the "What You'll Need" section, you'll still want to make sure to dress and pack appropriately.

Moderate trails are routes where you will likely work up a sweat, so you'll want to leave the street clothes at home or in the car. These are not technical hiking routes, and if you've got a solid pair of grippy shoes you'll probably be OK—especially on the fire road routes—but a decent pair of hiking-specific shoes will do you much better on these trails and the more difficult hikes.

Challenging trails are hikes that take a half day or longer, and for them you will definitely want to be in good shape, have actual hiking shoes, and be prepared to work up a good sweat. Even though some of the challenging routes in this book are short, they may have some steep or slippery sections or rough single-track trails.

There are only two **very challenging** hikes in the book, and—as you may have guessed—they are the most difficult. These routes traverse long sections of the park's trail network and involve steep climbs and potentially confusing

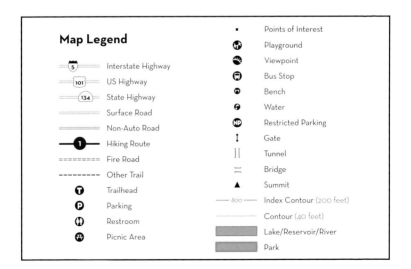

trail junctions in areas of the park that are not heavily traveled. Many hikers underestimate the trails in Griffith Park. Don't be one of them.

Almost every hike is located inside Griffith Park, so the rules and contacts are the same. If they differ, you'll see them here. You will find amenities nearby, GPS coordinates (in decimal degrees and based on the WGS84 datum) for the trailhead, and stuff you should know before you go, as well as how to get to the trailhead by car or transit where applicable. Because Griffith Park has several access points and L.A. is a huge city, there may be a better or faster route to these trailheads depending on where you're coming from.

I've also included icons for the following notable characteristics, which may help you pick your next hike. You can also see all of this information at a glance in the table at the front of the book.

Good for Kids: All kids are different, so you'll have to read the rest of the info to know if *your* particular kiddo is going to be OK, but if I think the trail may be worth your time, you'll see this icon.

Good Views: Trails with nice views—as long as the haze and/or marine layer cooperate—will be noted this way.

Historic Interest: Trails with fun, unique, or interesting stories or landmarks nearby will have this symbol.

Hollywood Sign: If you can get a nice view of the Hollywood Sign from the trail, you'll see this. No need to crowd all the lookie-loos on the same couple of spots, ya know?

Good Workout: A lot of the trails in Griffith Park have steep sections that will help you work up a sweat, but these routes are particularly good for it.

Solitude: Again, we're going to be speaking in relative terms here because, remember, you *are* in an urban park in a huge city, but these routes are more likely to give you some alone time along the way.

Transit Accessible: Check out these hikes if you want to leave your car at home. Be sure to read the descriptions—some hikes are only transit accessible at certain times or if you're hiking in certain directions. Also note that there are several hikes without this icon that *can* be done with transit but that may require some extra mileage on your shoes.

A scrub jay and a mockingbird enjoy the chaparral. (photo by Michael Nies)

TRAIL ETIQUETTE

Because this is a much-used urban wilderness park, please treat this land as a shared space and be considerate of others. You belong in this place, but this place does not belong to just you—so don't litter, don't smoke anywhere in the park *ever* (fires happen here every year), acknowledge others on the trail, and know the right of way: Hikers yield to equestrians; hikers should watch out for cyclists at trail crossings and on Vista Del Valle and Mount Hollywood Drives; and if both parties are on foot, hikers going uphill on a narrow trail have the right of way.

If you're hiking with a dog, keep it on leash everywhere in the park unless you're in the off-leash dog park, and bag and pick up poop. Please don't bag the poop and then leave the bag on the trail—that's not helping anything.

The Leave No Trace Center for Outdoor Ethics has an evolving list of seven principles that are good behaviors to follow and model for other folks on the trail who may not be aware of them. You can find more information about LNT practices and philosophy on www.lnt.org, but here's a summary:

1. **Plan ahead and prepare:** Don't just show up at a trailhead without knowing where you're going or without any food or water. Use this guidebook to find a route that's good for you, and make sure you and everyone who's joining you has what they need to stay comfortable on the trail.

2. **Travel and camp on durable surfaces:** Basically, stick to the established trail. As you'll find out, that's not always 100 percent possible in Griffith Park (see "The Trail Situation" just below), but you can help avoid unnecessary erosion and damage in the park by avoiding those undesignated user trails that seem to make straight shots up every ridge in the region.

3. **Dispose of waste properly:** Pack it in, pack it out. If you want to set an especially good example, bring an extra trash bag with you and pack out some litter you *didn't* pack in.

4. **Leave what you find:** Do not take anything from the park—not rocks, not plants, not animals, not wildflowers, *nothing* (OK, maybe if you're removing litter, that's cool). I have seen Instagrammers treating springtime trails as their personal bouquet stores or daybeds and— unbelievably—have even seen people pulling plants out of the volunteer gardens to take for themselves. Don't do that. Also, don't carve stuff in trees or benches or vandalize anything. I mean, come on.

5. **Minimize campfire impacts:** Campfires are prohibited in Griffith Park, so you should be good on this one, right?

6. **Respect wildlife:** You're going to encounter wildlife here—maybe just squirrels but also potentially rattlesnakes, coyotes, or bobcats. Leave the animals alone. Don't bother them, chase them, feed them, or try to take a sweet selfie with them for your social media feeds.

7. **Be considerate:** Remember, different folks enjoy this place for different reasons, so try to minimize your area of impact when you're out there. Know who has the right of way, try to keep your voices down, stick to the wide fire roads if you're hiking in a large group, and leave those obnoxious wireless speakers at home. Also, be friendly! Say hello to your fellow park goers—this is one of the few places in Los Angeles where people actually get to mingle and interact with each other.

THE TRAIL SITUATION

Ask five different local hikers what is and isn't a trail in Griffith Park and you'll get a dozen different answers. And someone's probably going to start yelling.

The question of what is and isn't an official trail in Griffith Park is somewhat of an ongoing debate . . . and the answers have changed over time. During the research for this book, I've consulted official park maps and publications from different time periods—and the number of discrepancies has been mind-boggling. Trails that are on the map in one decade disappear a few years later, even though they're still physically present. Names are swapped and changed, and trails that have one name on one map are called something else by another group with their own map. As you can imagine, these circumstances lead to a lot of confusion among park users.

Adding to the confusion is the fact that many trails that show up on the official map lack a designated name (and often trail signs), while some undesignated trails and firebreaks—manmade gaps in vegetation to help prevent the spread of wildfires—are in better shape than designated and named trails!

A NOTE ABOUT SAFETY

Safety is an important concern in all outdoor activities. No guidebook can alert you to every hazard or anticipate the limitations of every reader. Therefore, the descriptions of roads, trails, routes, and natural features in this book are not representations that a particular place or excursion will be safe for your party. When you follow any of the routes described in this book, you assume responsibility for your own safety. Under normal conditions, such excursions require the usual attention to traffic, road and trail conditions, weather, terrain, the capabilities of your party, and other factors. Because many of the lands in this book are subject to development and/or change of ownership, conditions may have changed since this book was written that make your use of some of these routes unwise. Always check for current conditions, obey posted private property signs, and avoid confrontations with property owners or managers. Keeping informed on current conditions and exercising common sense are the keys to a safe, enjoyable outing.

—Mountaineers Books

In 2016, the park installed much-needed trailhead and wayfinding signs and released a new official map (known as the 2016 Cartifact map to distinguish it from the many other maps of the park that have been released). For *Discovering Griffith Park*, I have taken great pains to generally stick to this official map. Where trails are designated as official on the map but are not named, I have not given them names but where appropriate, have noted colloquial names that are often used. In a few very rare cases, I've included some undesignated trails that I feel are in good enough shape and are useful enough to be of interest.

On the other hand, when you are in the park exploring the trails, you will most definitely see some "trails" that don't appear on maps in this book. In the vast majority of cases, these are unofficial routes and are often in very bad shape, meaning they're dangerous for hikers or they cause a substantial amount of erosion. As I was writing this book, several groups began a project to take inventory of the trails, and hopefully there will be an effort to eradicate

Bobcats (Lynx rufus) *are found in Griffith Park, but they're very elusive.* (photo by Robin Black)

problematic routes and use consistent names throughout the park, though I imagine that result will be several years away.

For the time being, know that most trails in Griffith Park are in the easy-to-moderate range. With a few exceptions, if you find yourself needing to use your hands to climb, standing on steep and exposed cliff edges, or putting yourself in danger, you are not on a designated trail.

Hikes at a Glance

Hike	Distance (miles)	Difficulty
1. Hollywood Reservoir	3.3	Easy
2. Lake Hollywood Park and Innsdale Trail	6	Moderate
3. Burbank and Cahuenga Peaks to Mount Lee	3	Challenging
4. Powerline Trail	2.6	Moderate
5. Hollyridge Trail	4.1	Moderate
6. Bronson Cave	0.6	Easy
7. Brush Canyon to Mount Lee	5.9	Moderate
8. Fern Dell	0.6	Easy
9. The Observatory Trails	1.9	Moderate
10. Loop, Western Canyon, and Berlin Forest Trails	2.7	Moderate
11. Mount Hollywood from The Trails Café	5.2	Moderate
12. Mount Hollywood from Charlie Turner Trailhead	2.1	Moderate
13. Bird Sanctuary Loop	0.4	Easy
14. Boy Scout Trail to Griffith Observatory	1.4	Moderate
15. Glendale Peak	3.2	Moderate
16. Hogback Loop	3.8	Challenging
17. Beacon Hill via Cadman Trailhead	3	Moderate
18. Fern Canyon to Lower Beacon	3.8	Moderate
19. Vista View Point from Cedar Grove	1.8	Moderate
20. Old Zoo Loop	1.9	Easy
21. Bee Rock Loop	2.8	Challenging
22. Amir's Garden	1.3	Easy
23. Mineral Wells Loop	4.2	Challenging
24. Toyon Canyon Loop	2.7	Moderate
25. North Peaks Loop	8	Very challenging
26. Griffith Peaks Traverse	7.6	Very challenging
27. Rattlesnake and Skyline Loop	3.2	Moderate
28. Oak Canyon Loop	3.2	Moderate
29. Royce's Canyon	3.4	Challenging
30. Mayor Cryer's Hike	4.8	Challenging
31. Mount Hollywood from the Old Zoo	5	Challenging
32. Cub to Caboose	5.1	Challenging
33. 3-Mile Trail	3.5	Moderate

Elevation Gain (feet)	Time (hours)	Good for Kids	Good Views	Historic Interest	Hollywood Sign	Good Workout	Solitude	Transit Access
80	1.5	•	•	•	•			
490	2.5		•		•			
1240	2.5		•		•	•		
630	1		•				•	
850	2.5		•					
60	0.5	•		•	•			
1330	2.5		•		•	•		
90	0.25	•		•				•
710	1		•		•	•		
700	2		•	•	•	•		
1010	2.5		•		•	•		
510	1.5		•		•	•		•
90	0.5	•		•			•	•
360	1	•	•		•			•
720	1.5		•			•	•	•
1160	2		•		•	•		•
910	1.5		•	•				•
720	2		•				•	•
560	1		•	•			•	•
330	1	•	•					•
730	2		•	•			•	•
410	1	•	•	•			•	
1060	1.5		•	•			•	•
700	1.5		•					•
2500	4		•			•	•	•
2120	4		•		•	•	•	
500	1.5		•	•				•
710	1.5		•				•	•
480	2		•			•	•	•
1400	2.5		•	•		•	•	•
1250	2.5		•	•	•	•		•
1370	2.5		•	•		•	•	•
600	2		•		•			•

1 HOLLYWOOD RESERVOIR

A calm trail with a unique view of the Hollywood Sign

Distance: 3.3 miles roundtrip
Elevation Gain: 80 feet
High Point: 790 feet
Difficulty: Easy
Time: 1.5 hours
Amenities: Porta-potties near the north gate and Weidlake Drive trailheads
GPS: 34.128867°N, 118.336321°W
Before You Go: Operated by L.A. Department of Water and Power; hours 6:30 AM to dusk except Thanksgiving, Christmas, and New Year's Day and some maintenance days; limited trail access and parking; dogs prohibited

GETTING THERE

PUBLIC TRANSIT At the time of writing, there are no transit connections.
DRIVING From the 101 northbound or Cahuenga Boulevard, head east on Barham Boulevard. Take a right onto Lake Hollywood Drive and stay on that road as it meanders through a residential neighborhood. At the signed intersection with Wonder View Drive, descend a hill toward the reservoir and park along the road, minding the parking restrictions. There is an alternate trailhead at the end of Weidlake Drive in Hollywood. Lake Hollywood Park has very limited street parking, and residents are already annoyed by tourists circling the block, so please park elsewhere!

There are a lot of ways to get a view of the world-famous Hollywood Sign—but only one includes a gentle stroll along the historic Mulholland Dam and Hollywood Reservoir under the sporadic cover of pine trees. Leave the crowds behind at the Griffith Observatory and Hollywood & Highland shopping complex, and join the locals on this popular walking and jogging path.

GET MOVING

Start out at the north gate of the Hollywood Reservoir (sometimes also called Lake Hollywood). Behind you, you may be able to see the Hollywood Sign at an odd angle, but don't strain your neck too much—you'll get much better views farther along this pleasant walk. Cahuenga and Burbank Peaks loom

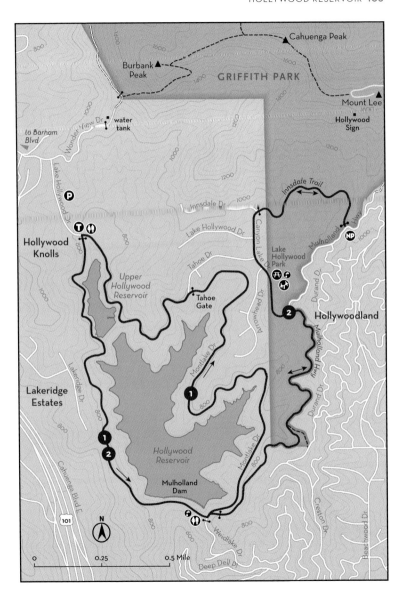

Be sure to look over the railings for the beautiful sculptures on the south side of the Mulholland Dam.

large behind you (Hike 3), and their rugged, rippling terrain is best appreciated in the early morning or late afternoon when shadows put eye-catching highlights on the east side of Cahuenga Pass.

Continue on the easy paved path as it hugs the western side of Upper Hollywood Reservoir. By 0.4 mile you'll pass the small upper dam and find yourself along the Hollywood Reservoir proper. Unique views of the Hollywood Sign begin to appear on your left—few people show off photos of the sign with palatial estates, towering trees, and a body of water in the foreground—but you may have to wiggle your camera's lens between gaps in the chain-link fence for a good shot.

If you don't feel like performing a chain-link peep show on the trail, just wait until you reach the Mulholland Dam at the 1-mile mark. As you cross this circa-1924 dam, you've got great views all over the place: to the north, the ridgeline running from Burbank and Cahuenga Peaks to Mount Lee—the

MULHOLLAND DAM AND THE SAINT FRANCIS DAM DISASTER

The Mulholland Dam (originally called the Weid Canyon Dam) is the last existing dam that William Mulholland designed and built—but it wasn't his final one. That distinction belongs to the infamous St. Francis Dam, situated north of Santa Clarita in San Francisquito Canyon. Construction on the St. Francis Dam began in 1924—the same year the Mulholland Dam was completed. Four years later on March 28, structural flaws in the St. Francis Dam led to a catastrophic collapse. The filled reservoir sent a 120-foot-high deluge down San Francisquito Canyon and into the Santa Clara River valley, where it swelled the riverbanks and flooded ranches and towns until it met the Pacific south of Ventura. At least 431 people died—still the second-largest loss of life in California history, after the 1906 San Francisco earthquake and fires. The disaster site became a national monument in 2019.

The St. Francis Dam disaster ruined Mulholland's name and career, and Angelenos began looking nervously up at the dam above the growing Hollywood neighborhood. Although several investigations found no structural flaws in the Mulholland Dam, engineers did determine the dam could use some reinforcement to increase uplift relief. In addition to keeping the reservoir well below its storage capacity, in 1933–34, workers placed 330,000 cubic yards of earth on the south face of the dam and planted trees and shrubs, effectively hiding the concrete structure from view of Hollywood residents. Out of sight, out of mind, right?

After the St. Francis Dam collapsed, the Mulholland Dam was reinforced—just in case.

iconic peaks of the more rugged side of Griffith Park. To the south: the center of historic Hollywood with buildings you've probably seen in dozens of movies and TV shows. Not to miss: the beautiful art deco bear-head sculptures visible from the south-facing rim of the dam.

Cross the dam, reaching the three-way intersection on the east side of the dam at 1.2 miles. The gate to Weidlake Drive is to your right, while a more rugged trail lies straight ahead past the gate on the dirt Mulholland Highway (Hike 2). Keep to the left to stay on Montlake Drive (closed to traffic). It's smooth, car-free hiking until you reach the Tahoe Drive gate at 2.6 miles. Stay straight to return to the north gate at 3.3 miles, staying on the worn dirt path along Lake Hollywood Drive or carefully sharing the road with lost tourists trying to drive to the Hollywood Sign in vain.

GO FARTHER

For a longer day on the trails—and probably the best front-facing views of the Hollywood Sign in Los Angeles—head onto the Mulholland Highway at the 1.2-mile mark and follow the directions for Hike 2. Just remember to get back to your car before parking restrictions take effect. Be quiet and courteous if you're walking along the residential streets to get back to the trailhead.

2   LAKE HOLLYWOOD PARK AND INNSDALE TRAIL

Walk through a historic neighborhood and enjoy some of the best front-facing views of the Hollywood Sign.

Distance: 6 miles roundtrip
Elevation Gain: 490 feet
High Point: 1070 feet
Difficulty: Moderate
Time: 2.5 hours
Amenities: Porta-potties at both Hollywood Reservoir trailheads; water, play area, and barbecue pits and picnic areas at Lake Hollywood Park
GPS: 34.128867°N, 118.336321°W
Before You Go: Operated by L.A. Department of Water and Power, L.A. Department of Recreation and Parks; lake trail hours 6:30 AM to dusk most days; dogs prohibited on lake trail but allowed on leash at Mulholland Highway and beyond

GETTING THERE
PUBLIC TRANSIT At the time of writing, there are no transit connections.
DRIVING From the 101 northbound or Cahuenga Boulevard, head east on Barham Boulevard. Take a right onto Lake Hollywood Drive and stay on that road as it winds through a residential neighborhood. At the signed intersection with Wonder View Drive, descend down the hill toward the reservoir and park along the road, minding the parking restrictions. There is an alternate trailhead at the end of Weidlake Drive in Hollywood. Lake Hollywood Park has very limited street parking, and residents are already annoyed by tourists circling the block, so please park elsewhere!

This hiking route may appear at first to be randomly assembled, but this fun saunter through the Hollywood Hills hits a lot of highlights in an oft-overlooked (and sometimes inaccessible) corner of the Griffith Park region. Enjoy an easy walk alongside a reservoir, then follow a surprisingly rugged trail—literally in the backyards of some of the houses of Hollywood royalty—before soaking in the best front-facing views of the Hollywood Sign in Griffith Park.

Be honest—you kind of want a selfie with the sign, don't you? Just be courteous to the folks who live nearby, OK?

FROM BILLBOARD TO EYESORE TO LANDMARK

Although the Hollywood Sign has been an iconic part of Los Angeles since its construction in 1923, its relationship with the city hasn't always been a mutual love affair. When the sign was first erected to advertise the new Hollywoodland housing development below it, it was never meant to be a permanent structure. A real estate boom in the early 1920s meant it was still financially feasible for the Hollywoodland developers not only to cut streets and level housing lots in narrow, winding canyons but also to put up 50-foot-tall letters lit by 4000 lightbulbs to advertise those housing lots. Initially, the letters lit up as *HOLLY*, then *WOOD*, then *LAND*, then all at once with a large white beacon marking the spot just below the letters. Very subtle. The builders didn't expect the sign to last more than eighteen months.

The initial developers of Hollywoodland wanted to build more houses—including atop Mount Lee—but the crash of 1929 put an end to those plans. The Great Depression encouraged the developers to donate some of the rougher terrain around Hollywoodland to the City of Los Angeles for annexation into Griffith Park.

The temporary sign fell into disrepair during the Depression and never really recovered. In 1949, a storm knocked down the *H*. The Los Angeles Department of Recreation and Parks wanted to tear down the sign and extend hiking and equestrian trails, but the Hollywood Chamber of Commerce adopted it that year, removed the *LAND*, and gave it a facelift. Even with some financial support, the sign was dilapidated again by the late 1970s. Wind and rain warped the first *O* and one of the *L*s was set on fire. Things weren't looking good for the ol' Hollywood Sign.

In 1977, the band Fleetwood Mac wanted to hold a benefit concert at the Hollywood Bowl to fundraise for a permanent sign upgrade, but nearby residents complained about the potential noise. So instead, *Playboy* founder Hugh Hefner pledged $27,777.77 to restore the letter *H* and asked fellow celebrities to chip in. By 1978, each letter had a sponsor (ranging from Gene Autry to Alice Cooper, who donated in memory of Groucho Marx), and a new metal sign was unveiled in time for Hollywood's seventy-fifth anniversary that year—with increased security around the sign to prevent access and potential vandalism.

GET MOVING

Follow the description for Hike 1 to the three-way intersection at 1.2 miles. Instead of keeping to the left to continue along the reservoir, stay straight to head up a slight paved incline. Pass a gate and you'll be on the dirt Mulholland Highway on the edge of a very narrow sliver of Griffith Park that hems in the western edge of the Hollywoodland neighborhood.

The chain-link fence on your left gives way to some sweeping views of the Mulholland Dam below you. Ahead, the trail meanders through some surprisingly dense chaparral and sage scrub in the shadow of historic mansions that housed early entertainment luminaries and other professional weirdos—and in many cases still do. *Dracula* star Bela Lugosi loved hiking up to the Hollywoodland Sign from his Tudor home with his Great Danes. *Brave New World* writer Aldous Huxley and his wife Laura held salons in their terraced gardens with Allen Ginsberg and Timothy Leary. Mobster Bugsy Siegel ran a speakeasy here during Prohibition, and the musician Moby lived in an iconic estate called the Wolf's Lair between 2010 and 2014 . . . where he likely baked some of his delicious vegan cookies. Which is all to say it's kind of fun to hike here and see little neighborhoody touches like tire swings and sculpture gardens along the way and wonder who put them there in the first place.

Keep left at 1.7 miles to continue north, ignoring the spur trail to Durand Drive in Hollywoodland. The Hollywood Sign looms large directly ahead—with an enormous Mediterranean estate hugging the hillside directly in front of it. You'll meet the walls of this estate around the 2-mile mark and walk on its driveway for a short distance (please be respectful!) before you hit Canyon Lake Drive at 2.2 miles. Carefully cross the street to enjoy this spectacular view of the Hollywood Sign, but don't fret if it's crowded—you'll have an even better view soon.

Turn left, descending on Canyon Lake Drive as it wraps around Lake Hollywood Park—a lovely open meadow below the Hollywood Sign that's been used as a dog park for more than a decade even though dogs are officially supposed to be on leash (the only off-leash dog park in Griffith Park is west of the Ferraro athletic fields). Canyon Lake Drive ascends a bit, passing Arrowhead, Tahoe, and Lake Hollywood Drives on the left before dead-ending at Innsdale Drive at 2.6 miles.

Head through the gate on the wide dirt Innsdale Trail and you're back inside Griffith Park and enjoying the closest front-facing views of the Hollywood Sign you can legally get. The Innsdale Trail ends back in Hollywoodland at the paved Mulholland Highway at the 3-mile mark. Return the way you came.

3 BURBANK AND CAHUENGA PEAKS TO MOUNT LEE

Get close to the Hollywood Sign and meet one of LA's celebrity trees on one of the best (and toughest) hikes in the park.

Distance: 3 miles roundtrip
Elevation Gain: 1240 feet
High Point: 1820 feet
Difficulty: Challenging
Time: 2.5 hours
Amenities: None, although the base of the Burbank Peak Trail may soon have toilets and trash cans
GPS: 34.132149°N, 118.337899°W
Before You Go: Increasingly popular trail; hike early or during the week to avoid crowds—and bring a trash bag to pick up litter

GETTING THERE

PUBLIC TRANSIT At the time of writing, there are no transit connections.
DRIVING From Barham Boulevard, head south on Wonder View Drive to the intersection of Lake Hollywood Drive, where limited parking is available. Do not drive east on Wonder View Drive past Lake Hollywood Drive—it is an extremely narrow dead-end residential street with no parking, and you are likely to make a lot of folks angry if you do.

Many trails inside Griffith Park are on fire roads and bridle trails, but if you're in the market for a solid single-track trail, this steep climb in the rugged western corner of the park is your best bet. You'll top out at the highest peak in Griffith Park, visit a celebrity tree with its own Instagram account, and end your journey right behind the Hollywood Sign.

GET MOVING

The first 0.2 mile of this hike is a walk on the paved Wonder View Drive, where you are not allowed to park. Although this dead-end street doesn't see a ton of traffic, remain alert and stick to the side of the road for your safety (and to let residents get in and out of their homes!). Please be on your best behavior in this residential neighborhood—you didn't bring a speaker with you, did you? Pass a gate and look toward the steep incline for a single-track trail at 0.3 mile.

A plaque used to mark this as the trailhead for the Burbank Peak Trail before it was vandalized, but the trail is easy enough to spot.

The Burbank Peak Trail kicks off with a steep and rocky climb up the dramatic east side of Cahuenga Pass. Many hikers underestimate how tough Griffith Park trails can be, but probably no trail is underestimated as much as this one. Do not attempt this hike in tennis shoes or sneakers, and especially don't do this hike without bringing water with you—it's short, but it's a serious trail.

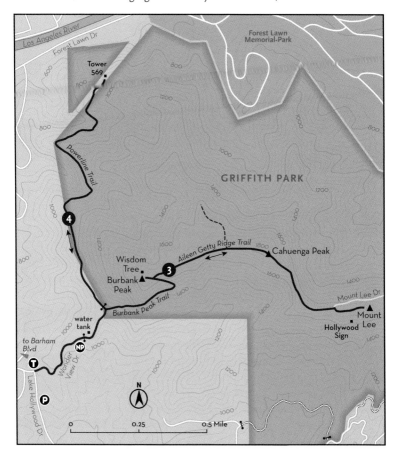

In Los Angeles, even a tree can be an Instagram influencer.

As you climb, take breaks to enjoy the sweeping views of the city. You should be able to spot the Hollywood Reservoir easily, and to the southeast are the Griffith Observatory and sometimes even downtown L.A. and beyond.

At 0.7 mile, you'll top out at the ridgeline. Head 0.1 mile west to visit what may be L.A.'s most famous tree, the Wisdom Tree, atop Burbank Peak. This tree was the sole surviving pine after a brushfire swept up the north side of the slope here in 2007, and it became a sort of hikers' shrine and pilgrimage spot. Visitors would leave snippets of paper with meditations, prayers, or headshots (it *is* L.A., after all). With the rise of social media, it's become more crowded and—unfortunately—sometimes seen as just a nifty backdrop for Instagram photos. Rock stacking has eroded the ground near its roots and people have been climbing and damaging its limbs—photos from several years ago reveal a much healthier-looking tree. Lately volunteers have taken to hauling mulch and water to its base to help keep it alive. Snap your selfie, knock down a rock stack, pick up some litter, and head back east along the Aileen Getty Ridge

HOW WE ALMOST RUINED CAHUENGA PEAK

Today, hikers love traversing the rugged trail from Burbank and Cahuenga Peaks to the backside of Mount Lee, and the iconic Wisdom Tree is a much-beloved presence in Griffith Park (it even has its own Instagram page, @the _wisdom_tree_la), but many don't know how precarious this area's status was.

In the 1940s the pilot-engineer-film-and-business tycoon Howard Hughes purchased Cahuenga Peak and 138 surrounding acres to build a palatial estate for his then-fiancée Ginger Rogers. But Rogers grew wary of Hughes's increasing . . . let's say . . . eccentricities (according to one account, Rogers told her friends she was worried Hughes would "hold her prisoner" atop Cahuenga Peak), and she called the whole thing off.

The property got lost in Hughes's increasingly large and complex business holdings, which found their way into various companies after his death in 1976. In a bit of typical L.A. real estate–flipping madness, a developer purchased the land from the Hughes estate in 2002 for $1.675 million, zoned four luxury estates, and put the property on the market in 2008 for $22 million.

Public outcry was loud and strong, and the Trust for Public Land announced an effort to raise $12.5 million to buy the land and add it to Griffith Park. Many Angelenos and park lovers donated to the cause. Last-minute donations from the Tiffany & Co. Foundation and *Playboy* magnate Hugh Hefner sealed the deal in 2010.

Without the efforts of the people who fought to it, protect this beautiful ridgeline could have easily been covered in giant houses for the super-wealthy.

Trail to Cahuenga Peak—the tallest mountain in Griffith Park. There is a small clearing at the summit at 1.2 miles, and the trail beyond this point gets even more challenging.

Just past Cahuenga Peak, carefully make your way down a short scramble to an unforgettably epic and narrow ridge between Cahuenga Peak and Mount Lee. From here, you'll be able to see down into the Forest Lawn Memorial-Park as well as soak in a sweeping panorama of the rugged and mercifully undeveloped terrain of the western park.

The trail rises and falls over a few steep and surprisingly tough bumps on the ridge, and at 1.5 miles you'll find a small clearing just south of the trail with plaques for Aileen Getty and *Playboy* magnate Hugh Hefner—a leading figure in the preservation of the Hollywood Sign as well as a 2010 advocate for protecting the land you're hiking on now from development. Just beyond this plaque, the trail spits you out onto paved Mount Lee Drive. Once you reach the road, keep right to walk behind the Hollywood Sign and to the summit of Mount Lee, where you are likely to be greeted by a diverse mix of tourists, runners, hikers, and confused travelers trying to figure out how to get a photo with the front of the sign. Return the way you came.

GO FARTHER
This route is also the first leg of the full-day Griffith Peaks Traverse (Hike 26).

4 POWERLINE TRAIL

Watch out for movie magic on a nearby studio lot in a rarely visited corner of the park.

Distance: 2.6 miles roundtrip
Elevation Gain: 630 feet
High Point: 1140 feet
Difficulty: Moderate
Time: 1 hour
Amenities: None, although the base of the Burbank Peak Trail may soon have toilets and trash cans
GPS: 34.132149°N, 118.337899°W
Before You Go: Increasingly popular trail; limited parking; hike early or during the week to avoid crowds

GETTING THERE
PUBLIC TRANSIT At the time of writing, there are no transit connections.
DRIVING From Barham Boulevard, head south on Wonder View Drive to the intersection of Lake Hollywood Drive, where limited parking is available. Do not drive east on Wonder View Drive past Lake Hollywood Drive—it is an extremely narrow dead-end residential street with no parking, and you are likely to make a lot of folks angry.

If approaching the Aileen Getty Ridge Trail gives you crowd-induced stress (and hey, on some weekends, I totally get it), consider taking the road less traveled. The lovely, rarely used Powerline Trail meanders along the western edge of Griffith Park before dead-ending near a powerline tower. If you're looking for some peace and quiet, this is a good place to go.

GET MOVING
Follow the directions for Hike 3 past the gate on Wonder View Drive (and remember to be courteous and conscientious to the folks who live there!).

Sage scrub can be exquisite in spring on the quiet Powerline Trail.

A GRIFFITH PARK GONDOLA?

From the Powerline Trail (Hike 4), hikers can enjoy the quiet and solitude of chaparral and sage scrub within view of the tourist attractions at Universal Studios. But that peace could become disturbed by a much more up-close tourist attraction—a gondola to the Hollywood Sign.

A 2018 study on transportation in and around Griffith Park called the Dixon Report had a slew of recommendations to alleviate increasing crowding and traffic. Some, like extended DASH lines and park-wide electric shuttles, make sense. Others—like building a second Hollywood Sign on the north side of Cahuenga Peak—are a bit sillier. But a recommendation to build a gondola from one of the nearby studios to either the summit of Mount Lee or a new viewing platform south of the Hollywood Sign caught a surprising amount of traction after Mayor Eric Garcetti pitched it as a potential revenue-generator in a TV interview.

A gondola here would require extensive development and intrusion into what is essentially the last corner of true urban wilderness in Griffith Park. In his 1910 book *Parks, Boulevards, and Playgrounds*, Griffith J. Griffith was pretty clear that developed attractions and manicured gardens were fine in certain areas but that we shouldn't forget that the true "playground" of the park was its rugged, undeveloped backcountry. Throughout its history, these two philosophical sides of the park have often been in conflict. Previous efforts to build gondolas and funicular railways inside the park have been stymied, but those who value the terrain in this region of the park will have to remain vigilant if they want this new gondola to join the previous efforts in history's dustbin.

When you see the Burbank Peak Trailhead—and its crowds—keep to the left to hike around an old chain-link gate.

Now you're on the Powerline Trail. This trail follows an old road grade that clearly hasn't been used as a road in quite some time—the broad path you're on gradually narrows into a single-track trail—all the while providing some truly unique views of the surrounding terrain.

Because this trail is significantly off the beaten path from most Griffith Park foot traffic, you'll get the chance to hike through some remarkably lush sage scrub, especially in years with wet winters. Dense groves of California sagebrush and long-blooming California buckwheats fill in the gaps between black sage, laurel sumac, and ceanothus. Late in spring, the hillsides may turn bright yellow from invasive black mustard as well as native brittlebushes and southern bush monkeyflowers.

If you're more attuned to the manmade attractions, this trail also offers up bird's-eye views of Universal and Warner Bros. Studios. You'll be able to clearly make out the backlots of both establishments, and if you bring some binoculars you might get to see a film or television shoot without having to know someone *who knows someone.*

The trail itself is pretty easy and simple to follow. As it narrows, you'll encounter some rough, eroded sections at 0.8 and 1.1 miles that require some careful maneuvering—but nothing too tough. If you're hiking a few days after a rainstorm, you may even get to see a small ephemeral waterfall at that first arroyo!

The trail ends at 1.3 miles at Tower 569. You may notice that some users have carved unofficial routes beyond the tower as well as up one of the arroyo drainages, but they are significantly rougher and more exposed than the trail you've been on and are not designed to curb erosion to the fragile terrain—so head back the way you came. If you're jonesing to head to the ridgeline above you, just take the route described in Hike 3 instead!

5   HOLLYRIDGE TRAIL

Reach one of the most popular Hollywood Sign viewing areas, despite a gate closure.

Distance: 4.1 miles roundtrip
Elevation Gain: 850 feet
High Point: 1250 feet
Difficulty: Moderate
Time: 2.5 hours
Amenities: Porta-potties at the end of Canyon Drive; two playgrounds and a picnic area nearby; drinking water near the playgrounds
GPS: 34.124480°N, 118.314251°W
Before You Go: Increasingly popular route to Hollywood Sign; limited parking; arrive early or take a rideshare; limited shade

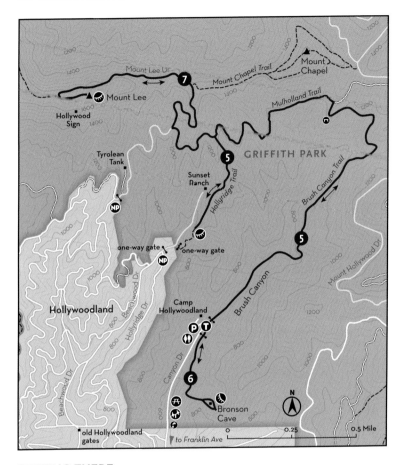

GETTING THERE

PUBLIC TRANSIT Efforts are being made to extend the DASH shuttle farther up Beachwood Canyon, but at the time of writing, there are no transit connections. **DRIVING** From Hollywood Boulevard, head north on Bronson Avenue. Keep left at 0.6 mile as Bronson becomes Canyon Drive. Continue driving until Canyon Drive ends. There are two trailhead parking areas and very limited street parking. Gates close at sunset.

Equestrians are a common sight on the Hollyridge Trail.

The Hollyridge Trail was formerly the quickest, easiest way to reach a solid viewpoint of the Hollywood Sign on foot—until in-car GPS and Google Maps directions funneled increasingly large crowds of tourists onto the narrow, hundred-plus-year-old streets of the Beachwood Canyon neighborhood. Residents were agitated, hikers were frustrated, and a nearby horse ranch sued the City of Los Angeles because people were blocking access to their stables. As a result of that lawsuit, the City locked the access gate in 2017. You can still reach that viewpoint—you just have to hike about seven times farther than you used to. But hey, you're in the mood for a good hike, right?

GET MOVING

Begin your hike at the end of Canyon Drive, heading north on the Brush Canyon Trail into Brush Canyon (this area is also commonly known as Bronson Canyon). Ignore the maintained road's sharp turn up at the gate toward Camp Hollywoodland.

THE MULHOLLAND HIGHWAY

Older maps sometimes call the dirt Mulholland Trail the Mulholland *Highway*—and indeed, you can still find stretches that are officially called that on the road's winding route toward the Hollywood Reservoir and west of Calabasas. Just to the west of Cahuenga Pass, you'll see Mulholland *Drive*.

In the 1920s, when L.A. was really getting into the habit of putting proto-freeways through all its parks (think: Elysian and MacArthur Parks), the plan was to pave Mulholland all the way across Mount Lee and connect it to Vermont Canyon Road at the same time Riverside Drive was paved along the Los Angeles River on the east side of the park. A housing boom in the Cahuenga Pass area intervened, stranding the eastern stretch of Mulholland as a dirt road. Riverside Drive eventually became the Golden State Freeway, eating up a large chunk of usable parkland and forever cutting off the park from easy access to the river.

The trail is lined by some impressive sycamore trees in these lower stretches, where a series of normally dry arroyos and washes meet near the bottom of Brush Canyon. You'll see a flood check dam on your right, and at about 0.3 mile the trail picks up its elevation gain. It's not especially steep, but it is steady and not very shaded, so you may do a bit of huffing and puffing during this stretch.

It's constant climbing until you reach a small bench rest stop at 1.1 miles. Along the way, the terrain keeps your views mostly inside Brush Canyon with glimpses of the east edge of Hollywoodland, but you'll also start to see the radio towers atop Mount Lee to the northwest. At 1.2 miles, keep left to head west on the Mulholland Trail.

The Mulholland Trail stays mostly level as it meanders along some ridgelines heading west. You'll have some wonderful city views south from here. On clear days you can make out the towers of Century City and sometimes Palos Verdes Peninsula and Catalina Island, too. You're also likely to pass some horseback tours from Sunset Ranch.

At 1.7 miles, keep left to begin on the Hollyridge Trail and make a slight descent as you head south. This part of the trail is almost exclusively traveled by horse, so the trail can be worn and sandy . . . which you may curse on the way back up. At the 2-mile mark, a small flat to the west of the Hollyridge Trail provides that spectacular viewpoint of the Hollywood Sign that everyone was clamoring to see—the towering white letters loom in the distance while the stables of Sunset Ranch sit in the foreground, giving the whole scene a "How the heck is this in L.A.?" sort of feeling. Return the way you came in, or continue to where the trail ends at that contentious gate. It opens one-way from the park to Beachwood Drive, where you can take your chances with ride-share services or walk down to the old Hollywoodland gates and hop on the DASH Beachwood Canyon shuttle.

GO FARTHER

A quick side trip to the Bronson Cave (Hike 6) is a great way to start or end this hike. If you're ambitious enough to hit the summit of Mount Lee, you've already done much of the legwork for Hike 7.

6 BRONSON CAVE

Visit an old quarry that you've definitely seen in TV and movies before—and venture into the original Batcave.

Distance: 0.6 mile roundtrip
Elevation Gain: 60 feet
High Point: 710 feet
Difficulty: Easy
Time: 0.5 hour
Amenities: Porta-potties at the end of Canyon Drive; two playgrounds and a picnic area nearby; drinking water near the playgrounds
GPS: 34.124480°N, 118.314251°W
Before You Go: Increasingly popular route to Hollywood Sign; limited parking; arrive early or take a rideshare; limited shade

GETTING THERE

PUBLIC TRANSIT At the time of writing, there are no transit connections.
DRIVING From Hollywood Boulevard, head north on Bronson Avenue. At 0.6 mile, keep left as Bronson becomes Canyon Drive. Continue driving until Canyon Drive ends. There are two trailhead parking areas and very limited street parking. Gates close at sunset.

I t should come as no surprise that a park so close to America's filmmaking epicenter would be featured in a lot of films and TV shows, but this short-and-easy hike to some unassuming old quarry scars brings you to a location that punches well above its weight—and offers a decent view of the Hollywood Sign, too. Take the kids for some outside time, then relax in the nearby playgrounds—or continue farther into the park for more of a hike.

GET MOVING

This hike begins at the north end of the paved Canyon Drive. To the north, the Brush Canyon Trail climbs toward the center of Griffith Park. To the west, a steep driveway ascends to Camp Hollywoodland—a popular girls-only campground and outdoor activity center (see the "Camping" section in "Other Outdoor Stuff" for more info). You'll want to make a sharp right-hand turn to start walking up a broad dirt fire road heading to the southeast.

Today, the canyon is generally pretty quiet, but if you were visiting in the early 1900s it would have been a much different scene. The Union Rock Company

Most people venture onto this trail for the Bronson Cave, but it also has a very unusual view of the Hollywood Sign.

operated a quarry here from 1903 through the late 1920s, hauling crushed rocks out of Brush Canyon for use in building roads, railways, and the port of San Pedro. When you turn to the east at 0.2 mile, you'll see the remains—deep scars in the canyon, some artificially flat sections, and a short branching tunnel that cuts right through a rock face.

Perhaps most famously known as the Batcave from the 1960s television series *Batman*, this area has been on-screen a shocking number of times, starting with 1919's *Lightning Bryce* and including films of almost every genre—*Star Trek VI*, *Invasion of the Body Snatchers*, *The Three Stooges Meet Hercules*, *Julius Caesar*, *Army of Darkness*, and *The Searchers* were all shot here, along with campy fare like *Teenagers from Outer Space*.

Hike through the cave—making sure to stomp around a bit to let any snoozing snakes know you're in the neighborhood. The trail loops around the outside of the cave on the other side after providing one of the park's loveliest views of the Hollywood Sign. Return the way you came in.

GO FARTHER

If you want more outdoor time, head south from the parking area to enjoy the large picnic area or playgrounds. If you're looking for longer hikes, this is also the trailhead for the Hollyridge Trail (Hike 5) and the route to Mount Lee from Brush Canyon (Hike 7).

7   BRUSH CANYON TO MOUNT LEE

The classic hiking route to the backside of the Hollywood Sign

Distance: 5.9 miles roundtrip
Elevation Gain: 1330 feet
High Point: 1710 feet
Difficulty: Moderate
Time: 2.5 hours
Amenities: Porta-potties at the end of Canyon Drive; two playgrounds and a picnic area nearby; drinking water near the playgrounds
GPS: 34.124480°N, 118.314251°W
Before You Go: Increasingly popular route to Hollywood Sign; limited parking; arrive early or take a rideshare; limited shade

GETTING THERE

PUBLIC TRANSIT At the time of writing, there are no transit connections.
DRIVING From Hollywood Boulevard, head north on Bronson Avenue. At 0.6
mile, keep left as Bronson becomes Canyon Drive. Continue driving until Canyon Drive ends. There are two trailhead parking areas and very limited street
parking. Gates close at sunset.

While it's not the shortest route to get up close and personal with the
backside of the Hollywood Sign, this is definitely the easiest and most
approachable one. A manageable but steady climb on dirt and paved roads
(closed to most automobile traffic) takes you behind a world landmark and up
to a perch with fantastic views of the city. It's easy to see why this route is so
popular with walkers, hikers, and trail runners!

GET MOVING

Follow the directions for the Hollyridge Trail route (Hike 5). At 1.7 miles, ignore
the Hollyridge Trail and keep to the right to continue hiking west on Mulholland Trail, and at about 2.1 miles, the dirt fire road you're on meets up with a
roughly paved Mount Lee Drive at a three-way intersection.

Mount Lee Drive is closed to public automobile traffic, although you may
encounter the occasional police or maintenance vehicle. If you want a short
side trip to see the front of the Hollywood Sign, keep left here to head toward
Tyrolean Tank (adds 0.8 mile roundtrip). If you're more of a behind-the-sign,
summit-seeking type, stay to the right to continue north.

Mount Lee Drive winds along some tight switchbacks as it rises toward the
long east-west ridge of Mount Lee, slowly revealing views to the north as it goes.
At 2.4 miles, ignore the single-track Mount Chapel Trail to the right and stay on
the road, which now bends west on the north side of Mount Lee. If it's clear,
you'll have some great views of the Verdugos and perhaps the San Gabriels
to the northeast and the Santa Susanas to the northwest. If not, you may spot
closer locations like Burbank, the Los Angeles River, or Walt Disney Studios.

At 2.8 miles, pass a plaque marking the Aileen Getty Ridge Trail (part of
Hike 3) and stay on the paved road as it winds its way behind the Hollywood
Sign, which you'll have to view through a chain-link fence. Do not attempt to

jump the fence or approach the sign—you would be quickly apprehended and ticketed. Instead, follow the road to the gated radio tower farm atop Mount Lee and look for a short dirt path to the summit plateau where everyone else is taking selfies. From this angle, you can crop out most of the chain-link fence, and on clear days you can see the L.A. sprawl all the way down to Long Beach and Catalina Island. It's often a crowded and popular route, but once you're standing here, you'll understand why it's worth the effort. Return the way you came.

Standing atop Mount Lee behind the Hollywood Sign is a rite of passage for hikers in L.A.

Historic, shady Fern Dell is probably the nicest way to enter the park.

8 FERN DELL

Walk through a beautifully shaded oasis steeped in history.

Distance: 0.6 mile roundtrip
Elevation Gain: 90 feet
High Point: 610 feet
Difficulty: Easy
Time: 0.25 hour
Amenities: Restrooms, water, and The Trails Café near north end of route
GPS: 34.109322°N, 118.307539°W

GETTING THERE

PUBLIC TRANSIT Bus lines 207, 180, 181, Rapid 780 and the B Line subway stop at Hollywood Boulevard and Western Avenue; DASH Hollywood stops at Western and Franklin Avenues. Walk north to the entrance of Fern Dell.

DRIVING Generally, parking is available in the Fern Dell area just north of Los Feliz Boulevard.

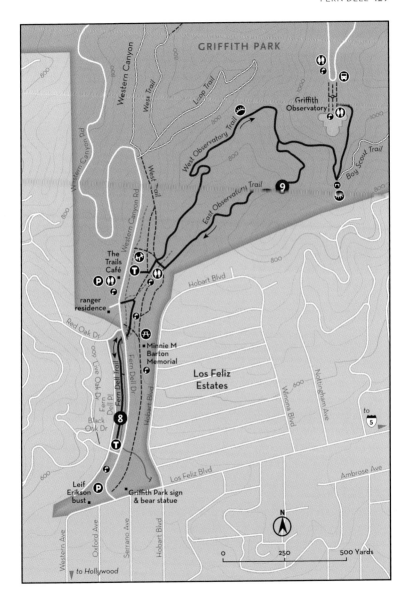

GRIFFITH PARK

Western Canyon

West Trail

Loop Trail

Western Canyon Rd

West Trail

Griffith
Observatory

West Observatory Trail

Boy Scout Trail

East Observatory Trail

9

Western Canyon Rd

The
Trails
Café

T

P

ranger
residence

Hobart Blvd

Red Oak Dr

Minnie M
Barton
Memorial

Fern Dell Dr

Fern Dell Trail

Los Feliz
Estates

Winona Blvd

Nottingham Ave

Live Oak Dr

Fern
Dell Pl

Black
Oak Dr

8

T

Hobart Blvd

to
5

Los Feliz Blvd

Ambrose Ave

Leif
Erikson
bust

P

Griffith Park sign
& bear statue

N

Western Ave

Oxford Ave

Serrano Ave

Hobart Blvd

0   250   500 Yards

to Hollywood

Mystery solved.

WHY IS THERE A STATUE OF LEIF ERIKSON IN THE PARK?

Just to the west of the intersection of Fern Dell Drive and Los Feliz Boulevard, curious hikers will note a stolid, stylized bust of the Viking explorer Leif Erikson. The statue's pedestal reads simply, "Leif Erikson—Explorer—Landed in America Year 1000."

L.A. is not often associated with Scandinavian culture, but in the 1920s and '30s, many Scandinavians immigrated to Southern California, including Iceland's first and most famous female sculptor, Nina Saemundsson. Born on a farm in rural Iceland in 1892, Saemundsson took up sculpting as a child and rose to international prominence. She moved to New York and created the famous *Spirit of Achievement* statue atop New York's Waldorf Astoria hotel and later moved to Los Angeles, where she appeared regularly in the *Los Angeles Times*. In 1934, she sculpted a statue of Prometheus outside her home in the Hollywood Hills with funding from

Don't be fooled by the distance. This short walk takes you through one of the loveliest corners of Griffith Park, where you'll find reliably flowing water, a lot of shade, and probably a photo shoot or two. This little trek also packs a surprising amount of history into its length and can be used as the start of longer hikes into the park or just a pleasant day sipping tea, having a picnic, or letting some little ones enjoy a playground.

GET MOVING

This route starts from the southern end of Fern Dell Drive—look for the large wooden sign that reads "Ferndell." Also be sure to note a sizable quartz stone with a plaque marking Los Angeles Historic-Cultural Monument #112—"A Gabrielino Indian Site."

the federal Public Works of Art Project. The City loved it so much, it funded a full statue for display in Westlake Park (now MacArthur Park) the following year. The statue still stands there today.

In 1936, Saemundsson was tapped by the Los Angeles Nordic Civic League to honor her ancestor Leif Erikson with this bust. The statue is only the third monument for the Norse navigator in the United States and was placed in Griffith Park in October 1936, accompanied by a Leif Erikson festival at the Los Angeles Breakfast Club.

The statue was a point of pride for L.A.'s Scandinavian community, which grew to support dozens of social clubs throughout the region. In 1952, members of the West L.A. Peer Gynt Lodge 6-22, Sons of Norway, formed the Leif Erikson Association to advocate for national recognition of Leif Erikson Day on October 9. The date was chosen to honor the arrival of the first ship of Norwegian immigrants to the United States in 1825 (and, let's face it, probably to compete with Columbus Day). The association went national several years later and is credited with helping achieve national recognition of Leif Erikson Day in 1964.

If passing by this statue piques your interest in the first European to stumble upon North America (let's not forget this statue stands *very* close to the site of a Tongva-Gabrielino settlement), the Peer Gynt Lodge 6-22 still meets the first Saturday of every month in Culver City. Their website notes, "You don't have to be Norwegian."

The council site known as Mokawee'nga (or Mocahuenga to the Spanish) was likely just a bit to the east—but it's the presence of reliable water that has made this general site so important to so many people over the years.

As you enter the Fern Dell area, you'll immediately note that stream of flowing water. This creek is born in nearby year-round springs. For the Tongva-Gabrielino, this water marked an important meeting ground for regional bands. Later, it was a source of irrigation water to Spanish and Mexican ranchers and drinking water for Anglo-Angelenos.

Proving that fad diets and New Age lifestyle brands helmed by Westside actresses are not new in L.A., Angelenos ascribed mystical qualities to the water here in Fern Dell. In 1929, a homeowner building a garage discovered a new spring, which was immediately dubbed "The Fern Dell Spa" by local newspapers . . . and the "Fountain of Youth" by other devotees. After that, people flocked from all over with empty jugs in hand to fill up on the supposedly healing water. By the 1960s, the well had become contaminated, and a deeper well was tapped and piped to drinking spigots near the Fern Dell Nature Museum (today a ranger residence).

Keep to the left—there are two broad paths that meander alongside the creek here, but the one on the west bank continues all the way to the end of the trail. There are several small, secluded offshoots of this main pathway, where you can take a seat on benches and enjoy the shade from native and climate-appropriate trees and plants—the shade here is strong enough to keep this area of the park about five to ten degrees cooler than other sections, even on the most brutal of sunny, hot days.

Look for a prominent, rocky, fountain-style sculpture on the west side of the trail as you make your way north—this is one of the rumored locations of the "Fountain of Youth" (the others are a spigot south of the Fern Dell entrance on Fern Dell Drive and the aforementioned nature museum). The Friends of Griffith Park are in the process of restoring some of the historic water infrastructure here as well as repairing the old fern gardens, which were installed as a demonstration of what the park could look like if more water was piped in to change the climate.

Outside of the wet seasons, the water in Fern Dell usually dries up around 0.2 mile, where the trail bends east and ducks under historic automobile and pedestrian bridges, but you can see how much farther up the irrigated landscape used to go—old cement bottoms of artificial lagoons and streams reach up toward the Observatory Trails and farther up Western Canyon. As restoration crews discover more of the original plumbing—some of it intact after all these years—there is talk of reactivating this section of upper Fern Dell to be more like its shadier, wetter lower half.

When you're ready, return the way you came.

GO FARTHER

This hike ends at the beginning of the East and West Observatory Trails (Hike 9) and West Trail, which can all be used to access the rest of Griffith Park.

9   THE OBSERVATORY TRAILS

One of the best ways to get to the Griffith Observatory on foot is also home to one of the best Hollywood Sign viewpoints.

Distance: 1.9 miles roundtrip
Elevation Gain: 710 feet
High Point: 1140 feet
Difficulty: Moderate
Time: 1 hour
Amenities: Restrooms and water at The Trails Café and Griffith Observatory; food at The Trails Café, inside the observatory, and occasionally outside it
GPS: 34.114586°N, 118.307137°W
Before You Go: Check www.griffithobservatory.org for hours and event schedules.

GETTING THERE

PUBLIC TRANSIT Bus lines 207, 180, 181, and Rapid 780 and the B Line subway stop at Hollywood Boulevard and Western Avenue; DASH Hollywood stops at Western and Franklin Avenues. Walk north to the entrance of Fern Dell (Hike 8) and continue on that trail until it ends near the trailhead for this hike. This adds about a mile to your hike each way. The DASH Observatory shuttle and Griffith Parkline stop at the observatory if you want to hike just one-way.

Griffith Observatory is an easily recognizable landmark visible throughout the park.

DRIVING From Los Feliz Boulevard, turn north on Fern Dell Drive. Park near The Trails Café for this hike.

Join hikers, walkers, trail runners, and urban explorers on one of the most popular routes to the historic Griffith Observatory. This loop route is also a wonderful place to get some views of the Hollywood Sign, enjoy spectacular sunsets, and avoid the nightmare of trying to park at the observatory itself.

GET MOVING

This hike begins across the street from The Trails Café—a wonderful place to start or end a hike, depending on how effectively you hike while full of pastries and tea. There are a few different ways to access the start of the trail, both north and south of the café, so just head to the east down into the old irrigated gullies of upper Fern Dell and look for the playground.

Several trails and fire roads meet up here—along with a number of unnamed and unofficial user trails. Head east of the playground and keep to the north. You'll see two broad fire roads snaking their way up toward the Griffith Observatory. To your left is the West Observatory Trail. To the right, it's the East Observatory Trail—a name that belonged to what is now the Boy Scout Trail until the park finally published official maps in 2016 (you may agree that *that* trail makes more sense to call "East Observatory Trail" since it's, you know, to the east of the observatory, but it won't be the last thing you encounter in Griffith Park that doesn't make sense!).

The trails are about the same distance, although the East Observatory Trail is more consistent with its elevation gain, while the west route goes in fits and starts. I find going up short, steep climbs to be easier than going down them, so I recommend climbing up the West Observatory Trail, but it's up to you. After one noticeably steep switchback at 0.3 mile, the West Observatory Trail flattens out on a ridge heading northeast that also happens to have one of the park's best (and least crowded) views of the Hollywood Sign.

Both Observatory Trails meet just after 0.6 mile. Head east to continue a steady climb as the fortresslike walls of the observatory rise to the north and stunning views of the city unfurl to the south. At 0.8 mile, you'll meet up with the Boy Scout Trail, an unofficial firebreak route to the south, and a dead-end fire road trail. You'll want to take the large, well-traveled fire road that continues climbing toward the observatory, which you'll reach at just about the 1-mile mark.

The Griffith Observatory is an incredible place to visit, so flip to "Museums and Cultural Attractions" in this book for more information. Even if you don't go inside, it's worth a stroll around the exterior and onto the rooftop, where views of the city, the San Gabriels, and the Verdugos are fantastic.

When you're ready, retrace your steps back down, and for a change of pace (and some lighter wear and tear on your knees), keep left at 1.4 miles to descend on the East Observatory Trail. Keep right at 1.8 miles to head toward the playground and back to the trailhead—and, oh yeah, those pastries at The Trails Café.

GO FARTHER

If you park near the Fern Dell entrance or take transit in, a stroll through Fern Dell (Hike 8) is an easy and lovely addition to this route. If you're in the mood for a longer day on the trail, head north of Griffith Observatory through the parking area (keep your wits about you—that area can get pretty crazy), where you can head to Mount Hollywood (Hike 12). Make an even larger loop by coming back down via the route described in Hike 11.

10 LOOP, WESTERN CANYON, AND BERLIN FOREST TRAILS

Avoid the traffic snarls on the way to the observatory— and get a workout.

Distance: 2.7 miles roundtrip
Elevation Gain: 700 feet
High Point: 1170 feet
Difficulty: Moderate
Time: 2 hours
Amenities: Water and restrooms along route (see map)
GPS: 34.117055°N, 118.306918°W

GETTING THERE

PUBLIC TRANSIT Bus lines 207, 180, 181, and Rapid 780 and the B Line subway stop at Hollywood Boulevard and Western Avenue; DASH Hollywood stops at Western and Franklin Avenues. Walk north to the entrance of Fern Dell (Hike 8)

Hillsides covered in blooming bigpod ceanothus (Ceanothus megacarpus) *are one of the earliest signs of spring in the park.*

and continue on that trail until it ends near the trailhead for this hike. This option adds about 1.1 miles to your hike each way.

DRIVING From Los Feliz Boulevard, head north on Fern Dell Drive as it becomes Western Canyon Road and park in the large parking area north of The Trails Café—right before the road makes a large switchback and climbs up toward the observatory.

I f you're trying to get to the Griffith Observatory and (wisely) don't want to drive, this combination of trails will get you there on one of the least congested routes in the popular southern section of the park. You'll take some lovely detours, enjoy terrific views along the way, visit a small pine forest gifted to L.A. from Berlin, Germany, have access to both the observatory and The Trails Café—and you'll save a significant amount of road rage by skipping the parking competition deeper inside the park.

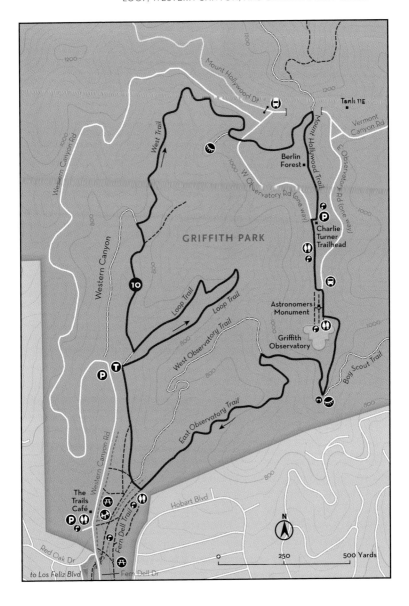

Mount Hollywood Dr

1200

1200

Tanls 11E

Vermont Canyon Rd

West Trail

1000

Western Canyon Rd

Berlin Forest

Mount Hollywood Trail

El Observatory Rd (one way)

W Observatory Rd (one way)

1000

1000

800

GRIFFITH PARK

Charlie Turner Trailhead

Western Canyon

10

800

Loop Trail

Loop Trail

Astronomers Monument

Griffith Observatory

West Observatory Trail

800

Boy Scout Trail

800

P T

East Observatory Trail

800

The Trails Café

Western Canyon Rd

Hobart Blvd

P

N

Fern Dell Trail

Red Oak Dr

0   250   500 Yards

to Los Feliz Blvd

Fern Dell Dr

The Astronomers Monument outside the observatory

GET MOVING

From the parking area, cross Western Canyon Road and look for the Loop Trail near a barely noticeable flood control dam (if you're not hiking in the wet season, you'll probably just see an odd, densely forested miniature valley). Head east to hike on the Loop Trail—a lovely little side trip into a dense grove of ceanothus, oaks, and sycamores. It's one of the quietest places in this part of Griffith. At 0.3 mile, the Loop Trail winds back toward the west. You'll most likely see tourists snapping selfies above you at the Griffith Observatory parking area. You may also spot a few errant user trails climbing into the brush to who knows where—don't be fooled into thinking they'll get you to the observatory.

Instead, enjoy the stroll back to near your trailhead, keeping right at 0.6 mile to head on the West Trail toward the Berlin Forest. It's a broad fire road with a gentle climb through more old oak and sycamore trees—keep eyes and ears alert for birds and coyotes. In the wet season, the drainage basin that feeds the creek in Fern Dell is sometimes flowing up here, but most of the year it remains dry but shaded.

At 0.8 mile, ignore the dead-end trail on the right-hand side, and then stay to the right at the junction. The trail loses most of its shade here and the incline increases, so if you're hiking in the warmer months, try to tackle this section in the morning or early evening to avoid the worst heat. At 1.1 miles, you'll start to get some great views looking down Western Canyon—at 1.2 miles, there's a short spur you can take to a good viewpoint where you can make out Century City and Santa Monica on clear days.

Cross West Observatory Road at 1.3 miles and continue a steep climb through a forest that was burned in a 2018 fire. Keep right at 1.4 miles to head south on the Mount Hollywood Trail through the Berlin Forest (thankfully, spared from that fire). The Berlin Forest was planted by visiting dignitaries from West Berlin when the two municipalities became sister cities, and new trees are still sometimes planted by visiting diplomats today. Enjoy the views and shade, then continue hiking south toward the Charlie Turner Trailhead at 1.6 miles.

Carefully cross the observatory parking area and cross the lawn in front of the *Astronomers Monument* to descend toward Fern Dell on the Observatory Trails. Keep right just before the 2-mile mark and stay on the wide fire road trail, and at 2.1 miles, keep left to use the East Observatory Trail to descend to the playground across from The Trails Café (the West Observatory Trail will get you there, too, but its steeper slope isn't as friendly on the knees coming downhill). Keep right at the playground just past 2.5 miles to head north back to your trailhead.

GO FARTHER

This trailhead is also great for hiking to Mount Hollywood (follow the guide for Hike 11 for a gentle climb and Hike 12 for a slightly tougher one).

11 MOUNT HOLLYWOOD FROM THE TRAILS CAFÉ

Perhaps the best way to summit Mount Hollywood from Western Canyon—plus there's coffee (and tea) at the trailhead.

Distance: 5.2 miles roundtrip
Elevation Gain: 1010 feet
High Point: 1625 feet
Difficulty: Moderate
Time: 2.5 hours
Amenities: Restrooms, water, and even food along this route (see map)
GPS: 34.113895°N, 118.307485°W

GETTING THERE

PUBLIC TRANSIT If you feel like adding an extra 0.9 mile each way to this hike, you can take the Metro B Line subway or bus lines 207, 180, 181, or Rapid 780 to Hollywood Boulevard and Western Avenue, or DASH Hollywood to Western and Franklin Avenues. Walk north on Western and follow directions for Hike 8 through Fern Dell to this trailhead.

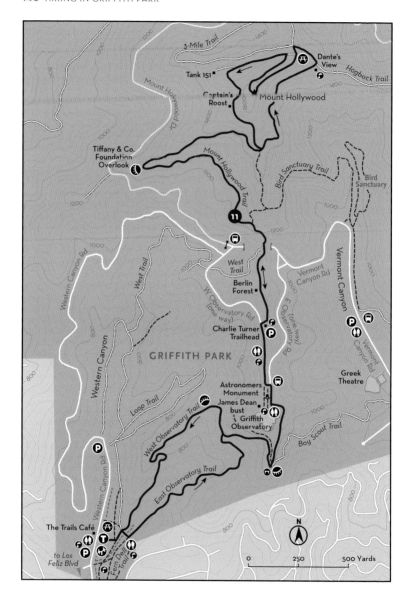

The Trails Café is a great place to load up on carbs and/or caffeine before or after a hike.

DRIVING From Los Feliz Boulevard, turn north on Fern Dell Drive and drive north 0.4 mile. There is parking along Fern Dell Drive and a larger lot just to the north of The Trails Café.

Wouldn't it be nice to start your hike with some coffee? Or maybe end it with a refreshing iced tea? This is an iconic and popular hiking route in Griffith Park for many reasons: you reach the summit of Mount Hollywood and pass the Griffith Observatory, it's on mostly well-graded fire roads with only a few steep sections, and the views are great the entire way—but having the trailhead across the street from the beloved The Trails Café makes this route to the top of Mount Hollywood a winner, even if you *do* manage to resist one of their lavender shortbread cookies.

GET MOVING

Get your caffeine on (or scope out the menu for your post-hike reward) at The Trails Café, and then cross the street. There are a few different trail entrances, so just aim for the playground. Continue east past the restrooms and veer right to hike on the East Observatory Trail. Both the west and east trails will get you to the same spot with about the same amount of distance, but the East Observatory Trail has a milder ascent. Keep right at 0.5 mile and left at 0.7 mile to continue your climb to the Griffith Observatory, which you'll reach at 0.9 mile (see "Museums and Cultural Attractions" for more info). If you'd like, cross the lawn between the observatory and the *Astronomers Monument* for a bust of James Dean and a view of the Hollywood Sign, or just head north across the lawn toward the oft-crowded area of buses and tourists.

At about the 1-mile mark, carefully cross the parking lot to the Charlie Turner Trailhead and keep hiking north on the Mount Hollywood Trail toward Berlin Forest, and at 1.3 miles stay straight to cross an overpass of the observatory roads, then stay on the broad fire road to continue on the Mount Hollywood Trail (a steeper, shorter option is described in Hike 12).

It's a gentle, almost imperceptible incline. Ignore the frustrating switchback slowly getting filled in with sage scrub just past 1.5 miles, and at 1.7 miles you'll reach the Tiffany & Co. Foundation Overlook, one of the better official viewpoints of the Hollywood Sign. Keep trucking up the Mount Hollywood Trail and at 2 miles you'll reach a large trail junction. Looking south from here it's almost a straight line to the observatory, which is a pretty neat view—but it gets better!

Ignore the very unofficial and highly eroded user trail that climbs up Mount Hollywood, and continue hiking straight ahead to meet the Hogback Trail at Dante's View at 2.3 miles. Grab some water if you need it, and check out the incredible views to the north of the park. Then hike west and keep left to reach the summit of Mount Hollywood at 2.6 miles.

When you're done admiring the view, head down the north side of Mount Hollywood but keep to the left at 2.7 miles and again shortly after to dodge a dead-end route to Tank 151. At about 2.9 miles, you'll pass Captain's Roost, currently being restored after a 2007 wildfire (see the "Volunteer Gardens and Special Forests" section in "Other Outdoor Stuff" for more on the Berlin Forest, Dante's View, and Captain's Roost).

Keep right at 3.1 miles to return the way you came. At 4.6 miles, keep right for a change of scenery and a great Hollywood Sign viewpoint on the West Observatory Trail—but if you have creaky knees or don't like steep descents, I'd recommend coming back down the East Observatory Trail instead.

GO FARTHER

An alternate ascent or descent can be made via the West Trail between The Trails Café and Berlin Forest, which you can follow on Hike 10.

Absorb beautiful views of Los Angeles from the summit of Mount Hollywood.

12 MOUNT HOLLYWOOD FROM CHARLIE TURNER TRAILHEAD

This quick and dirty route to the summit of Mount Hollywood is a classic L.A. hike.

Distance: 2.1 miles roundtrip
Elevation Gain: 510 feet
High Point: 1625 feet
Difficulty: Moderate
Time: 1.5 hours
Amenities: Water and restrooms at trailhead; water at Dante's View
GPS: 34.120739°N, 118.300412°W
Before You Go: Lot parking limited during free hours; strictly enforced during paid hours; go early, take DASH Observatory shuttle, or hike in

GETTING THERE

PUBLIC TRANSIT The DASH Observatory shuttle is by far the easiest and least aggravating way to get to the Charlie Turner Trailhead. It runs during the hours that parking requires a fee, and the shuttle will connect you to the Los Feliz

neighborhood and the Vermont/Sunset B Line subway station. Check www.ladot
transit.com for schedules and fares. The Griffith Parkline runs here on weekends
for free.

DRIVING You're gonna brave it, huh? From Los Feliz Boulevard, take either Fern
Dell Drive, Vermont Avenue, or Hillhurst Avenue to the observatory. Parking at
the Charlie Turner Trailhead/Griffith Observatory lot is sparse and expensive—
after 10:00 AM on weekends and noon on weekdays, you'll be paying $8 an hour,
as of the time of writing. As the day goes on, you'll be fighting with tourists,
buses, and selfie snappers. I'll say it again: If you're driving, go early—we're
talking sunrise-hike early. The park opens at 5:00 AM.

Mount Hollywood isn't the tallest peak in Griffith Park, but it is certainly
one of the most popular. This route to the summit from the Charlie
Turner Trailhead is the shortest way to get to those killer views—and it's an
iconic and beloved way to start or end your day. If you hike to this peak at sunrise or sunset often enough, you'll start to see and recognize the regulars—
who sometimes include marathon trainers, old-timer trail vets who'll leave you
in the dust, dog walkers, people walkers, *bird* walkers (for real), boxers in those
weird plastic sweat suits, and even a former or current L.A. city councilperson
or mayor. The prime minister of Canada was spotted up here a few years ago,
too! This hike has got a fun small town feel for being in the second biggest
city in the US.

GET MOVING

From the Charlie Turner Trailhead—named for a longtime caretaker of Dante's View—head north on the Mount Hollywood Trail. You'll pass a trail map,

*Charlie Turner was an important figure
in the park's volunteer history.*

where I guarantee you will see at least
one tourist group in the process of
realizing the Hollywood Sign is not on
Mount Hollywood.

Reach the Berlin Forest at 0.1 mile.
Stay straight at the junction with the
West Trail at 0.2 mile to cross over the
tunnel for auto traffic. Here's where
it can get a little tricky—look for a

single-track trail departing from the right-hand side of the Mount Hollywood Trail, but you're looking for one that *isn't* a crazy straight shot up an eroded, dangerous hillside. The designated trail here is not marked, and there are several user trails nearby, so look for the one that begins with some clear steps cut into the stone and take that one.

After you turn, you'll parallel the Mount Hollywood Trail for a short bit, then take a steep switchback east at 0.3 mile and hit a junction with the Bird Sanctuary

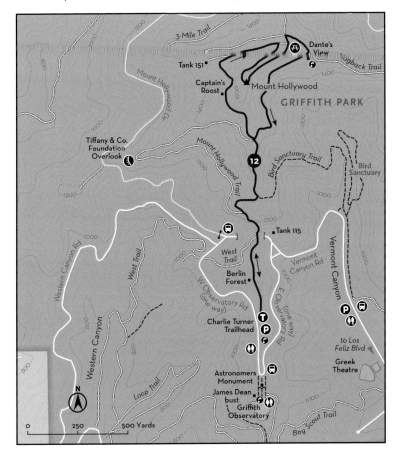

Trail shortly afterward. Keep to the left to head north (again, the trail you're on here should *not* be super steep   watch out for and avoid user trails!) and you'll reunite with the Mount Hollywood Trail at a four-way junction at 0.5 mile.

You can reach the summit on either uphill path of the Mount Hollywood Trail (a firebreak that became an unofficial route to the summit has been badly eroded, and the park is discouraging people from using it), but for this route head clockwise by keeping to the left. At 0.6 mile you'll pass the Captain's Roost garden—badly burned in a 2007 fire but on the mend thanks to volunteer caretakers. Stay to the right just before 0.8 mile and again just before 0.9 mile to stay on the clear route to the summit of Mount Hollywood.

Enjoy the views, then continue clockwise on the Mount Hollywood Trail by keeping to the right as you descend on the north slope. Pass a small picnic area and stay right at 1.2 miles to head toward the Hogback Trail. Just before 1.3 miles you'll hit Dante's View, which has water and another nice opportunity to stroll one of Griffith Park's volunteer gardens.

Head south on the Mount Hollywood Trail from Dante's View, and just before 1.6 miles, you'll close the loop. Head back down to the Charlie Turner Trailhead the way you came in.

GO FARTHER

If the single-track trails have you spooked, no need to worry—simply stay on the Mount Hollywood Trail instead! You can follow the directions from the Charlie Turner Trailhead in Hike 11.

13 BIRD SANCTUARY LOOP

More coyotes than people travel these trails wedged between two of the park's busiest attractions.

Distance: 0.4 mile roundtrip
Elevation Gain: 90 feet
High Point: 1000 feet
Difficulty: Easy
Time: 0.5 hour
Amenities: Water and restrooms at trailhead
GPS: 34.124361°N, 118.297070°W
Before You Go: Limited parking and bus access during Greek Theatre events—check www.lagreektheatre.com for schedule; dogs prohibited in the bird sanctuary

GETTING THERE

PUBLIC TRANSIT The DASH Observatory shuttle and Griffith Parkline stop at the Greek Theatre, which is an easy 0.4-mile walk from the trailhead.

DRIVING From Los Feliz Boulevard, head north on Vermont Avenue or Hillhurst Avenue toward the Greek Theatre. (Hillhurst feeds into Vermont Avenue, which becomes Vermont Canyon Road just before the theater.) There is a parking area located just to the west of the trailhead on Vermont Canyon Road, past

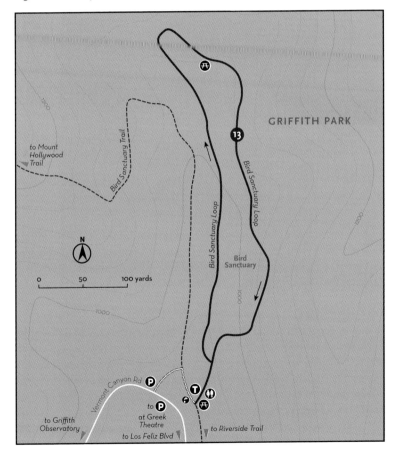

Listen closely for the hammering of acorn woodpeckers (Melanerpes formicivorus), or look for their stored food in notches in the trees. (photo by Sheri Cohen)

the Greek Theater, but the lot is very small. There is a larger lot just to the south of the bird sanctuary, across the street from the Riverside Trailhead.

Hike through one of the earliest developments in the Vermont Canyon area of Griffith Park on a peaceful, rarely visited loop trail. The historic bird sanctuary has seen better days but still gives visitors a chance to see (and listen to) the park's wildlife away from the bustle of more popular nearby trails.

GET MOVING

This nice, short, and simple stroll begins at the old bird sanctuary gates at the north end of Vermont Canyon Road. You will note a water fountain, restroom, and picnic tables near the outer entrance—as well as some exceptional historic stonework. The bird sanctuary itself is surrounded by a light chain-link fence that is open during park hours—for this hike, don't go up the Bird Sanctuary *Trail* directly to the west of the sanctuary itself.

In the 1920s, Griffith J. Griffith's son, Van, actively pushed for improvements to Griffith Park as a member of the board of park commissioners. He saw

GET THEM TO THE GREEK, EVENTUALLY

In 1913, still stinging from his new persona non grata status in the city after returning from prison, Griffith J. Griffith offered to pay for a grand theater in Vermont Canyon. At first, plans proceeded quickly—Griffith even got famous soprano Ellen Beach Yaw to roam around Vermont Canyon singing to determine which site had the best acoustics (side note, look up her rendition of "The Skylark" on YouTube if you want to hear some incredible vocal gymnastics). The mayor and the city council agreed to Griffith's plans, but political infighting tied construction up until after Griffith's death. While the theater was under construction, a wildfire almost destroyed the entire structure, but it opened in September of 1930.

The early stuffy classical theater fare and Works Progress Administration (WPA) marionette shows have given way to flashy pop concerts, and today seeing a show at the Greek is something of a rite of passage for Angelenos—watching your favorite artist as the setting sun casts its alpenglow on the peaks of Griffith Park can be a truly magical experience.

Head to www.lagreektheatre.com for schedules and tickets.

The Greek is one of the best performance venues in Los Angeles.

Vermont Canyon as the new main entrance to the park and wanted a number of developed attractions here, including a zoo, campgrounds, and Pacific Electric Red Car service (the widened median strip of Vermont was as far as that project went). Opposition from neighborhood residents eventually whittled those plans down to the quieter improvements, like a popular bird sanctuary.

As you enter, keep to the left of the sanctuary's lone loop trail to hike in a clockwise direction. The broad trail meanders alongside an old, artificial, rock-lined creek as it makes a slight incline. If you visited the bird sanctuary in earlier days, you may not recognize the scenery now—a 1979 hiking feature in the *Los Angeles Times* describes the sanctuary as having "the feeling of being in the mountains, following a burbling stream as it gently flows from dell to dell." Then, the irrigated canyon was full of nonnative trees and felt more like Fern Dell.

The 2007 Griffith Park Fire tore through the southeastern corner of the park, and most of the nonnative trees in the bird sanctuary were lost. The upside of this loss was that the area was closed long enough for the native sage scrub and chaparral to make its way back into the sanctuary. Today, you're more likely to enjoy sycamores, sumacs, and sages than coast redwoods, but a few of the old pine trees did survive. Volunteers have replanted some trees and tidied up the old irrigation systems, and in 2019 they began a multistage habitat restoration using native plants grown from seeds gathered inside Griffith Park. You can expect this area to look even better as those plants get established over the next few years.

You'll reach the back of the sanctuary at 0.2 mile, where the trail turns east near a beautifully situated picnic table and then turns south. As you head back toward the trailhead, remember to tread softly and quietly and you just might catch some of the wildlife living in such close proximity to city dwellers. I've seen woodpeckers, scrub jays, ravens, and red-tailed hawks in the skies and on branches here—and a few coyotes sharing the trail with me, too.

GO FARTHER

The bird sanctuary is an easy, gentle add-on to the more intense Hogback Loop (Hike 16). You can also make a nice loop up to Griffith Observatory from the Bird Sanctuary Trail, heading south on the Mount Hollywood Trail to the Charlie Turner Trailhead and then returning to the Greek Theatre on the Boy Scout Trail.

14 BOY SCOUT TRAIL TO GRIFFITH OBSERVATORY

Use this transit-accessible way to hike to the observatory when Vermont Canyon Road gets stuffed with traffic.

Distance: 1.4 miles roundtrip
Elevation Gain: 360 feet
High Point: 1140 feet
Difficulty: Moderate
Time: 1 hour
Amenities: Restrooms and water
GPS: 34.118590°N, 118.294520°W
Before You Go: Limited parking and bus access during Greek Theatre events—check www.lagreektheatre.com for schedule

GETTING THERE

PUBLIC TRANSIT The DASH Observatory shuttle and Griffith Parkline stop at Commonwealth Canyon Drive.

DRIVING From Los Feliz Boulevard, head north on Vermont Avenue or Hillhurst Avenue. There is a parking lot at Vermont Canyon Road and Commonwealth

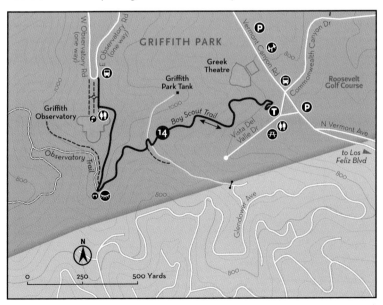

Canyon Drive. More parking is available along Vermont Canyon Road and Vista Del Valle Drive near the picnic area.

If you want to take transit into the park but still want to get your blood pumping to get up to Griffith Observatory, the Boy Scout Trail is your best bet. Climbing up a sometimes steep but mostly moderate fire road from the Greek Theatre, this route offers up some beautiful city views and occasional views of the old houses of Los Feliz, too. It's great for a quick out-and-back, an alternative to observatory traffic, an add-on to make a larger loop, or a sunset hike with a transit connection!

GET MOVING

From the intersection of Vermont Canyon Road and Vista Del Valle Drive, head west and look for the broad fire road climbing quickly from the north side of the street. This is the Boy Scout Trail, formerly known as the East Observatory Trail on older maps (which makes more sense to me, but hey).

Although this route is fairly gradual in its incline, the initial kickoff is steep—so don't be dismayed if you're huffing and puffing near the trailhead. This trail is pretty straightforward, too: Just past 0.3 mile, the trail makes a slight turn northward and crosses a paved access road to the Griffith Park Tank to the north—jog quickly to the right when you reach the paved road and you'll find

On clear days it's easy to appreciate the huge scope of Los Angeles.

the broad trail continuing to the west just beyond some brush. You can also follow this road south to a gate that will put you into the Los Feliz neighborhood on Glendower Avenue, a lovely place to explore quietly and politely. I recommend bringing an urban hiking book like Charles Fleming's *Secret Stairs* or Bob Inman's *Finding Los Angeles by Foot*, though.

At the half-mile mark, you'll meet up with the Observatory Trail coming from the west at an epic viewpoint looking southward on the never-ending city of Los Angeles unfurling toward the ports at Long Beach and San Pedro. To the north, that temple of science known as Griffith Observatory looms above you—this is one of the most impressive angles to view it from.

Head north and you'll reach the observatory grounds at 0.7 mile. Enjoy the exhibits, gaze at the stars, and return the way you came.

GO FARTHER

You can easily build your own loop around the southern portions of the park here—the terrain is hilly and offers solid routes for hikers and trail runners looking to build a little sweat. Head down either of the Observatory Trails toward The Trails Café, then head north on the West Trail to the Berlin Forest (Hike 10) and turn south to the observatory to complete the loop. Or head north through the observatory parking lot to the Charlie Turner Trailhead and continue on to Mount Hollywood (Hike 11 or Hike 12), or follow Hike 33 to end up at another DASH Observatory and Parkline stop to return to the transit system.

15 GLENDALE PEAK

Climb a short and rugged trail to a secluded summit off a popular trail.

Distance: 3.2 miles roundtrip
Elevation Gain: 720 feet
High Point: 1184 feet
Difficulty: Moderate
Time: 1.5 hours
Amenities: Restrooms south of the trailhead near the Greek Theatre
GPS: 34.121796°N, 118.296820°W
Before You Go: Limited parking and bus access during Greek Theatre events—check www.lagreektheatre.com for schedule

GETTING THERE

PUBLIC TRANSIT The DASH Observatory shuttle and Griffith Parkline stop just south of the trailhead at the Greek Theatre. The DASH is accessible via several stops in the Los Feliz neighborhood and at the Vermont/Sunset subway station.
DRIVING From Los Feliz Boulevard, head north on Vermont Avenue for 0.7 mile. The trailhead is located on the east side of Vermont Canyon Road, just across the street from the parking lot north of the Greek Theatre.

The southern region of Griffith Park is not known for its quiet or seclusion, but just a short distance off one of the most popular workout routes in the park, those in the know can experience both qualities at rarely visited Glendale Peak. On clear days, enjoy nearly 360-degree panoramic views from the San Gabriels to the Pacific Ocean here—and great views of downtown, too.

GET MOVING

This trail begins at the Riverside Trailhead on a wide fire road that heads to the southeast on a sharp angle from Vermont Canyon Road. Although you start off with a steep climb, the terrain levels out a bit before 0.2 mile as the trail swings to the north.

Glendale Peak gets surprisingly few visitors.

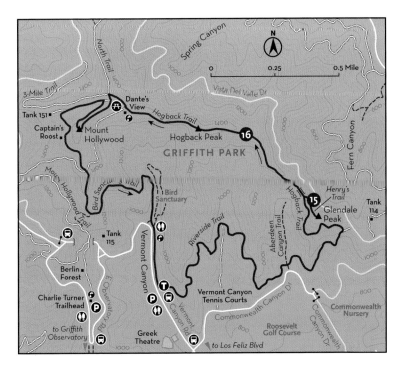

Almost right away, you'll have some nice views into the seating area of the Greek, and if it's clear you should start to see some of the skyscrapers of downtown peeking out from behind the hills, too. Just before 0.5 mile, stay straight to continue on the Riverside Trail, ignoring the fire road connecting to Commonwealth Canyon Drive and the tennis courts to the south and steering clear of the unofficial user trail that heads north.

At 0.9 mile, the trail drops down again near another short connector trail to Commonwealth Canyon Drive and a dead-end trail that heads north into Aberdeen Canyon. Stretch out your legs, then stay on the wide fire road with the steep ascent as it climbs up to the northeast, away from Commonwealth Canyon Drive.

At 1.2 miles, take a sharp left at the intersection with the paved Vista Del Valle Drive to continue on the fire road Hogback Trail, which hugs the southern face of Glendale Peak and swings north again. The Griffith Observatory comes into view to the west, and the links of Roosevelt Golf Course are more visible now that you've got some elevation under your legs.

At 1.5 miles, you'll see a seemingly out-of-place bridge on the Hogback Trail, placed there after a fire made the ridgeline too unstable for safe hiking. Look for a small blue sign ringed with cacti that points you in the direction of Glendale Peak via Henry's Trail. Henry's Trail was named for Henry Shamma, a Sierra Club hike leader who brought countless groups to this perch in the park and tirelessly maintained the trails nearby.

Henry's Trail climbs up some steep stairs to the ridgeline of Glendale Peak and reaches the marked summit at 1.6 miles. The views here are some of the best in the park, especially for a summit that doesn't see a whole lot of foot traffic. Return to the trailhead the way you came in.

GO FARTHER

For a longer trail day and a tougher workout, continue back to the Hogback Trail and keep right to follow the route for the Hogback Loop (Hike 16).

16 HOGBACK LOOP

Work up a sweat on this classic fitness loop with steep inclines and rustic single-track trails.

Distance: 3.8 miles roundtrip
Elevation Gain: 1160 feet
High Point: 1625 feet
Difficulty: Challenging
Time: 2 hours
Amenities: Water and restrooms along route
GPS: 34.121796°N, 118.296820°W
Before You Go: Limited parking and bus access during Greek Theatre events—check www.lagreektheatre.com for schedule

GETTING THERE

PUBLIC TRANSIT The DASH Observatory shuttle and Griffith Parkline stop just south of the trailhead at the Greek Theatre. The DASH is accessible via several stops in the Los Feliz neighborhood and at the Vermont/Sunset subway station.

Once you cross the footbridge on the Hogback Trail, get ready to climb.

DRIVING From Los Feliz Boulevard, head north on Vermont Avenue for 0.7 mile. The trailhead is located on the east side of Vermont Canyon Road, just across the street from the parking lot north of the Greek Theatre.

The Hogback Loop is one of the most popular fitness hikes in Los Angeles. As you rise above the city on the sometimes-exposed Hogback Trail, the views are epic, the sense of accomplishment is palpable, and the sweat is real. This loop trail tacks on the nearby summit of Mount Hollywood for good measure before coming down the rugged, single-track Bird Sanctuary Trail. On warm days, start early or wait until it cools off to avoid overheating—there's almost no shade on this route.

GET MOVING
From the Riverside Trailhead, follow the directions for Glendale Peak (Hike 15) to the junction with Henry's Trail at 1.5 miles. From here, keep to the left

to cross the footbridge across an exceptionally narrow section of the ridgeline and continue on the Hogback Trail.

The Hogback Trail past Glendale Peak narrows a bit but still remains a relatively wide footpath. Now, though, it's noticeably steeper than what you've been on so far—and in certain sections it's fairly exposed to steep drop-offs on either side. You'll want to make sure you're wearing shoes with good traction, as the dry and dusty terrain can sometimes be a lot more slippery than you'd expect it to be.

Dodge the trail runners and other fit folks as you make your way west, remembering to take some time to enjoy some of the most exceptional views you can get in this corner of the park. It's a great place to really take in the full scale of Griffith Park and the L.A. region in general.

Just before the 1.9-mile mark, you'll climb a small bump that some maps mark as Hogback Peak (the name and the peak are not well-known, but it's still fun to be aware of). Ignore the user trails to the south here and continue west, where you will keep on climbing toward the backside of Mount Hollywood. Pass Dante's View and its welcome water fountain at 2.1 miles, then keep left at the junction with the North Trail for a quick side trip to the summit of Mount Hollywood.

Head down the west side of Mount Hollywood through the Captain's Roost and keep south at the four-way junction before 2.9 miles to make a beeline toward the observatory. Keep left at the junction just past the 3-mile mark, to head east down the single-track Bird Sanctuary Trail, and you'll be standing in front of the actual bird sanctuary (Hike 13) at 3.6 miles. Follow the path on the east side of Vermont Canyon Road to return to the Riverside Trailhead.

GO FARTHER

For some extra trail time, skip the Bird Sanctuary Trail at the 3-mile mark and instead continue descending to the west to return to the Mount Hollywood Trail. Continue south through the Berlin Forest and Charlie Turner Trailhead to the Observatory Trails, then descend east to the Greek Theatre via the Boy Scout Trail and walk back to the trailhead along Vermont Canyon Road. This loop puts an extra 0.8 mile on your personal odometer.

17 BEACON HILL VIA CADMAN TRAILHEAD

*A serene hike to the
easternmost peak
of the Santa Monica
Mountains*

Distance: 3 miles roundtrip
Elevation Gain: 910 feet
High Point: 1001 feet
Difficulty: Moderate
Time: 1.5 hours
Amenities: None
GPS: 34.118249°N, 118.273720°W
Before You Go: Be courteous when parking in this residential neighborhood; Cadman Drive is a narrow dead end, so park on Griffith Park Boulevard instead.

GETTING THERE

PUBLIC TRANSIT Metro buses 96, 180, 181, Rapid 780, and the Griffith Parkline stop near the Mulholland Memorial Fountain, which is about 0.4 mile from the trailhead. Walk west on Los Feliz Boulevard and north on Lambeth Street to Griffith Park Boulevard. Metro bus 96 and the Griffith Parkline stop at the Griffith Park Pony Rides and Griffith Park & Southern Railroad, which is an alternate trailhead.

DRIVING From Los Feliz Boulevard, head north on Griffith Park Boulevard. The trailhead is at the intersection of Griffith Park Boulevard, Shannon Road, and Cadman Drive. Street parking is limited, but the route can also be accessed from the parking lot near the Griffith Park Pony Rides and Griffith Park & Southern Railroad.

Hike the peaceful, relatively quiet Cadman and Coolidge Trails to the summit of Beacon Hill—the easternmost peak in the Santa Monica Mountains—for phenomenal views of the city and nearby mountains. In earlier times, this summit held a literal beacon to guide airplanes flying in and out of the old Griffith Aviation Park.

GET MOVING

Begin at the intersection of Griffith Park Boulevard, Shannon Road, and Cadman Drive. Griffith Park Boulevard dead-ends straight ahead of you—veer to the left to walk on Cadman. There are no sidewalks here and the street is narrow, so even though it's a short dead-end street, be sure to keep an eye and ear out for

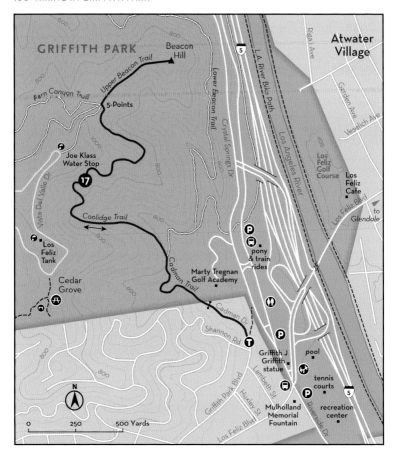

cars. The pavement of Cadman ends at 0.2 mile, where you'll pass through a gate and into Griffith Park proper.

Ignore the two user trails to your left near the 0.3-mile mark as the partially shaded trail wraps its way around the Marty Tregnan Golf Academy to the east. Just past the 0.4-mile mark, keep left to start climbing on the Coolidge Trail (if you had to park down near the train and pony rides, you'll meet up with this route from the Lower Beacon Trail here).

HOLD THE MUSTARD

Following a good rainy season, many beautiful plants in the park stretch out with vigorous new green growth and showy blooms. In the southeastern corner, which was scarred by the 2007 Griffith Park Fire, you are likely to see entire hillsides covered by tall leafy stalks with small yellow flowers.

Although this flower-filled view may be visually appealing, the plant you're looking at is black mustard (*Brassica nigra*), a highly invasive weed that is a major problem all over Southern California. Black mustard grows quickly and crowds out natives that would otherwise take root. It can sprawl into trails and usually dries up and dies by the summer, leaving a mess of flammable material behind just in time for wildfire season.

Biologists in the Santa Monica Mountains acknowledge it is nearly impossible to eradicate black mustard from the region, but with vigilance and a lot of effort, it can be kept under control. Check with the volunteer groups of the L.A. Department of Recreation and Parks or the Friends of Griffith Park to find out if there are any weed-control events scheduled, or offer to plan one yourself.

While it makes for nice photos when it blooms in spring, black mustard prevents native plants from taking root.

Looking south along the L.A. River and 5 freeway toward Silver Lake and downtown

The shade thins out past here as you start to climb up the ridges to the south of Beacon Hill, but the views will also improve significantly. You'll get better views of the golf academy, sure, but you'll also start to get some great views of the San Gabriel Mountains. Keep going up, and soon you'll spot the Silver Lake neighborhood, downtown Los Angeles, and the twin ribbons of the Los Angeles River and the 5 freeway snaking through the river's former non-concrete-bound channel. On exceptionally clear days, you might even be able to see prominent Santiago Peak down in Orange County, too.

At 1.3 miles, the trail meets up with several other routes at a location known as 5-Points. Keep to the right to follow the Upper Beacon Trail—a very clear, steep fire road that heads to the summit of Beacon Hill. A few quick, steep bumps and you'll be standing at the summit at 1.5 miles, where you can vaguely make out the remnants of the foundation of the beacon for the airfield for Griffith Aviation Park. It was said that pilots could only take off if they could see the beacon from the airstrip—and it also helped prevent pilots from crashing into the hill.

The views from here can be truly spectacular—especially after a good winter rainstorm has cleared the air. You may be able to make out peaks in the Verdugos and San Gabriels and see all the way down to Catalina Island if you're lucky.

You may think you see some faint trails heading down from the summit, but they're unofficial (and incredibly steep) user trails that are not maintained or approved by the park. Using them can cause more erosion, so give the mountain a break and return to Cadman Drive the way you came in.

GO FARTHER
You can do a full loop around the base of Beacon Hill instead of returning directly back to the trailhead. Just follow the directions in in Hike 18.

18 FERN CANYON TO LOWER BEACON

Exceptional views and beautiful springtime blooms in the park's southeast corner

Distance: 3.8 miles roundtrip
Elevation Gain: 720 feet
High Point: 1001 feet
Difficulty: Moderate
Time: 2 hours
Amenities: None
GPS: 34.131212°N, 118.282690°W

GETTING THERE
PUBLIC TRANSIT Metro bus 96 and the Griffith Parkline stop at Crystal Springs Drive near the Park Film Office and the visitor center, which is a short walk from the trailhead.

DRIVING From Los Feliz Boulevard, head north on Crystal Springs Drive. Turn left at the visitor center toward the merry-go-round and park in Lot One. The trailhead is at the gated access road just before the parking lot.

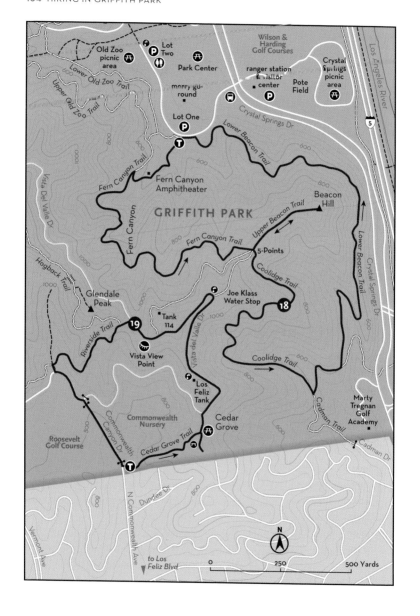

This alternate approach to the summit of Beacon Hill uses the significantly easier parking infrastructure inside the park. Surprisingly, this beautiful, view-packed route is still relatively lightly traveled. Soak in ceanothus blooms in spring and a native butterfly garden on the way up as well as exceptional views along the Los Angeles River basin on the way down.

GET MOVING

Head to the south end of Lot One and look for the gate. Head west on the south side of the road. As you head west, you'll see a flood control dam. Keep to the left to start on the Fern Canyon Trail, then keep your eye out for a narrow footpath that heads into the grove of coast live oaks. Keep left again here to step onto the Fern Canyon Nature Trail.

This short side trip is a lovely detour from the wider Fern Canyon Trail. The Friends of Griffith Park have planted and cared for a number of California native plants here, many of which are marked. You'll see California sagebrush, laurel sumac, purple sage, and shade-loving lemonade berry. In the late winter, you're also likely to spot chilicothe (wild cucumber) vines sprawling out and covering everything with white blossoms before they produce their otherworldly seedpods. Most of these plants attract butterflies and hummingbirds, so if you hike quietly here, you've got a great chance at spotting wildlife.

Ignore the user trails heading south, and at 0.2 mile you'll pass through the Fern Canyon Amphitheater. Hike up a short incline to the Fern Canyon Trail and keep to the left to start your climb up to Beacon Hill. This meandering fire road winds its way through dense groves of bigpod ceanothus—a sturdy evergreen bush that looks nondescript for most of the year but absolutely explodes in white blooms midwinter. It's one of the surest early signs of spring in Southern California.

The trail makes a few bends as it gains elevation and turns toward the east, reaching the upper end of Fern Canyon and providing some spectacular views toward Glendale and the Verdugos and San Gabriels. Keen-eyed hikers looking southwest toward Glendale Peak may even be able to spot the small footbridge on the Hogback Trail.

At 1.2 miles, you'll reach the junction of 5-Points. There are a lot of options from here, but keep to the left to head to Beacon Hill on the Upper Beacon Trail. This fire road gets pretty steep, but it's a short huff to the top of the easternmost

The iconic pyramid-shape of Beacon Hill and the rain-swollen Los Angeles River seen from just south of Los Feliz Boulevard

of the Santa Monica Mountains. Soak in the views, then backtrack to 5-Points and keep left to head down on the Coolidge Trail.

By 2.4 miles, the Coolidge Trail meets up at a three-way junction with the Cadman Trail and Lower Beacon Trail. Keep left to head north on the Lower Beacon Trail, which wraps around the edge of the Marty Tregnan Golf Academy (watch out for flying golf balls!). At 2.5 miles, keep left to stay on the Lower Beacon Trail—the spur trail to the right heads down to the pony and train rides and alternate parking.

At 2.9 miles, ignore the user trail up to Beacon Hill and continue north. The trail here parallels Crystal Springs Drive, the 5 freeway, and the Los Angeles River . . . and while you may think a trail near a freeway sounds like an awful thing, the views are actually pretty fantastic—you get a great, sweeping view of the San Gabriels and can clearly see where the soft bottom of the L.A. River has allowed life to return.

At 3.2 miles, the trail turns west, away from the freeway. Here, you'll have fantastic top-down views of the Crystal Springs picnic area—and one last bit of elevation gain before you drop back down to the trailhead.

19 VISTA VIEW POINT FROM CEDAR GROVE

Hike through a historic nursery and pine-sheltered picnic area to a beloved viewpoint.

Distance: 1.8 miles roundtrip
Elevation Gain: 560 feet
High Point: 1098 feet
Difficulty: Moderate
Time: 1 hour
Amenities: Water fountains (with dog-friendly spouts!) along the route
GPS: 34.118475°N, 118.286156°W

GETTING THERE

PUBLIC TRANSIT Metro bus 180/181 stops at Los Feliz Boulevard and Commonwealth Avenue, an easy half-mile walk to the trailhead. The DASH Observatory and DASH Los Feliz shuttles also stop one block west at Los Feliz Boulevard and Hillhurst Avenue and may run more frequently than 180/181.

DRIVING From Los Feliz Boulevard, head north on Commonwealth Avenue. Park on Commonwealth Avenue north of Dundee Drive, making sure to pay attention to parking restrictions. Remember, you are in a residential neighborhood. Note that it is not possible to drive on Commonwealth Canyon Drive past the Commonwealth Nursery.

This short but stunning loop trail in a surprisingly quiet corner of Griffith Park starts out tough but rewards all who travel it. Kick your legs into gear with a steep climb to the peaceful, forested Cedar Grove picnic area, then loop around to the locals' favorite Vista View Point and back down around the historic Commonwealth Nursery. You'll have exceptional views almost every step of the way and a lot of options to extend your trip, too.

GET MOVING

At the north end of Commonwealth Avenue, just after the street crosses into parkland, you'll spot a small sign mounted on a pole denoting Los Angeles Historic-Cultural Monument #942—Griffith Park. Keep to the east side of the street and look for a break in the fence with some signs displaying park rules (and a helpful poop bag dispenser for your four-legged friends). Through the

Young native plants soak up the sun at the revived Commonwealth Nursery.

FROM REFORESTATION TO RESTORATION

Historically, Griffith Park caretakers have been just as interested in altering the park as in preserving it. One example has been the pervading desire to make the chaparral and sage scrub of the region into something it isn't—a lush, wet forest.

The idea to heavily irrigate the park was first proposed in the 1910s by Superintendent Frank Shearer, who envisioned a tropical Griffith Park fed by irrigation sprinklers. Shearer encouraged the City of Los Angeles to secure water rights near Western Canyon and spearheaded the development of Fern Dell as a demonstration garden for what the rest of the park could look like.

When Van Griffith became a parks commissioner in the 1920s, he took up the mantle of "Reforestation." The thinking was that chaparral and sage scrub were dangerously fire prone, so replacing them with pine and oak trees would be safer for the encroaching neighborhoods. At the time, Los Angeles mayor George Cryer was an avid hiker in Griffith Park and supporter of reforestation, so he helped secure funds to move the Municipal Nursery from Elysian Park to the end of Commonwealth Avenue in 1927.

Within a year and a half, this nursery was growing around 2 million plants for parks throughout the city. But when John C. Porter replaced Cryer in 1929, he butted heads with Griffith on reforestation. Griffith resigned from the parks commission in protest. The nursery limped along until it closed in the 1970s.

Plans to irrigate Griffith Park peaked in 1968, when the Department of Water and Power said if they were able to build reclamation plants, Griffith Park could receive the water equivalent of 60 inches of rainfall per year—basically the precipitation of hurricane-prone Miami. A mind-boggling plan proposed 40 (!) lakes in Griffith Park, along with 10 (!!) waterfalls, and a 500-foot-tall cascade on Mount Hollywood (!!!).

Today, saner minds prevail, and the Commonwealth Nursery is slowly coming back to life—this time, dedicated to California native and climate-appropriate plants. Although it's not open to the public at the time of writing, it houses a joint project with groups including Grown in LA, Los Angeles Department of Recreation and Parks, Los Angeles Parks Foundation, Los Angeles Conservation Corps, and City Plants. The nursery is being envisioned as an urban environmental learning center, complete with research plots, demonstration gardens, and a seed bank for California native plants for use in public projects throughout the region.

Keep tabs on current and future projects at www.growninla.org.

gnarled oak trees, you'll spot a rough-looking, somewhat vague series of paths that head toward the hillside. This is the Cedar Grove Trail.

This route doesn't wait to warm up and throws some steep elevation gain at you right away. That's the bad news. The good news is that almost immediately, you'll have some stunning views of the varied houses in the neighborhood, which range from Spanish Colonial Revival to Mediterranean villas to sprawling midcentury ranch houses and hulking modernist cubes. If you're in the mood for something more art deco monumental, just look west—you'll have a solid view of the Griffith Observatory perched above the city. In the early spring, invasive black mustard blooms here send up tiny yellow flowers, while native brittlebush provides a nicer contrast with larger sunflower-style blooms.

At the 0.2-mile mark, ignore some user trails near a bench and keep left to dive into a dense grove of laurel sumac. In this shady stretch, look for exotic periwinkle flowers providing a splash of purple along the forest floor.

You'll emerge into the surprisingly expansive, surprisingly forested Cedar Grove picnic area. It is popular as a quick-and-easy stand-in for cooler climes; don't be surprised if you stumble upon a film, television, or commercial shoot here. A network of trails meanders through the area. Keep to the left, and at 0.3 mile take a right for a quick spur to some picnic tables and a bench with a million-dollar view of Central and West L.A.

Head north when you're done, and at 0.4 mile take a right onto paved Vista Del Valle Drive. The hike is much smoother sailing from here on out, so expect to see more runners, walkers, and families as the paved road gently loops and rises to the north, opening up some stunning views of downtown L.A. and the San Gabriels and Verdugos. On exceptionally clear days, you may even be able to see the tallest peaks in Southern California—from north to south, Mount San Antonio (Mount Baldy), Mount San Gorgonio, and Mount San Jacinto. The prominent peak farther to the south, if you can see it, is Santiago Peak—the highest in the Santa Ana Mountains.

A TV crew sets up their shot near Cedar Grove.

You'll pass the Los Feliz Tank on the left at 0.6 mile, artfully painted to blend into the landscape. There's a water fountain and usually a dog bowl or two nearby. If you miss it, don't fret—you'll hit the Joe Klass Water Stop at 0.8 mile, where you'll find another fountain along with picnic tables and some hitching posts for horses to complement the spectacular views.

Keep heading west on Vista Del Valle from the water stop, passing by Tank 114 on the north side of the road. At 1.1 miles, you'll find yourself on the broad, paved Vista View Point, commonly known to most locals as the Griffith Park Helipad. This sweeping viewpoint is rightfully popular and especially beautiful at sunrise and sunset. Continue west on Vista Del Valle and keep to the far left at 1.2 miles to descend on the Riverside Trail. Keep left at 1.5 miles to hike on the side of Commonwealth Canyon Drive back to the trailhead. The road is closed to through-traffic but is still traveled by maintenance vehicles and vans carting those film crews around, so keep an eye out as you hike back.

GO FARTHER

For a more substantial trail day, keep right at the 1.2-mile mark to join the Hogback Trail heading toward Mount Hollywood, and follow the directions for Hike 16.

20 OLD ZOO LOOP

Explore the ruins of the old L.A. Zoo—now a lively picnic area.

Distance: 1.9 miles roundtrip
Elevation Gain: 330 feet
High Point: 720 feet
Difficulty: Easy
Time: 1 hour
Amenities: Water and restrooms at Old Zoo picnic area
GPS: 34.131212°N, 118.282690°W
Before You Go: Free Shakespeare Festival in the Old Zoo picnic area early some evenings in summer

GETTING THERE

PUBLIC TRANSIT Metro bus 96 and the Griffith Parkline stop at Crystal Springs Drive near the Park Film Office and the visitor center, which is a short walk from the trailhead.

DRIVING From Los Feliz Boulevard, head north on Crystal Springs Drive and take a left at the Park Film Office to head toward the merry-go-round. Park in Lot One. The trailhead is at the gated access road just before the parking lot.

There's a good chance you may have seen the Old L.A. Zoo already. Perhaps best known for appearing in *Anchorman: The Legend of Ron Burgundy*, these eerily abandoned zoo grounds have been featured in many films and television shows—and have been the backdrop of many an aspiring actor's headshots, too. After sitting vacant and vandalized for many years, this newly revitalized

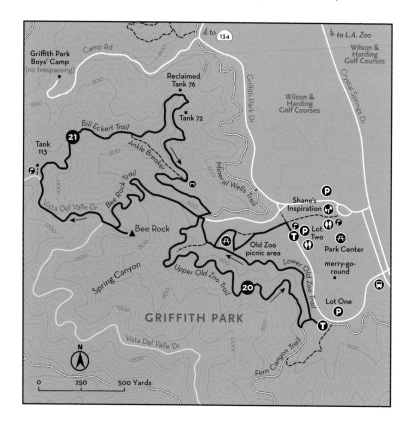

picnic space is still rough enough around the edges to feel a little creepy and weird but established enough to host annual Shakespeare performances.

GET MOVING

Although you can reach the center of the Old Zoo ruins with a shorter walk from Lot Two, this route begins at Lot One to take you through the outer ruins of the zoo—and it's got more of a fun, "whoa, here's the Old Zoo!" vibe when you get to the picnic area. From the south end of Lot One, hike west on the paved road, ignoring the Fern Canyon Nature Trail and keeping right at the flood control dam to go up an unmarked fire road. Keep right at 0.1 mile to turn onto the Lower Old Zoo Trail.

This route makes some gentle inclines as it meanders along the ridges toward what some old maps used to call Ostrich Farm Canyon. The parking lot where you started this route is near the site of an ostrich farm owned by naturalist Dr. Charles Sketchley that was considered a thrilling tourist attraction of its time. Seeing the appeal of the farm on his land, Griffith went into business with Sketchley and Moses L. Wickes to build a narrow-gauge railway to the farm from downtown Los Angeles near Beaudry Avenue and Sunset Boulevard. Sketchley got visitors. Griffith got to show off his real estate subdivisions and explore some early ideas about parks, recreation, and transit connections.

As you continue along the trail, eventually you'll start to see some remnants of cages and zoo infrastructure—at first through chain-link fences and later up close and personal. Just before 0.5 mile, the trail descends to the Old Zoo picnic area, and here's where you'll really start to see some of the cool stuff. Keep right when you reach the paved path at the bottom of the Lower Old Zoo Trail to walk counterclockwise around the picnic areas. You'll see cages and ruins that used to be aviaries and homes for tigers, lions, and bears that are now home to picnickers, oddity lovers, and self-styled social media "influencers."

Depending on park budgets and the perseverance of graffiti types, the zoo grounds can have a range of appearances from fascinating to terrifying, but over the past few years it's happily leaned more toward the former. Stay on the paved path and complete a counterclockwise loop around the broad meadow area (home to a future stage for the Independent Shakespeare Co.). Continue following the paved path west, walking past more old zoo cages and another lovely picnic area near a seasonal arroyo.

At 0.9 mile, look for an opening in the chain-link fence, then keep to the left onto the Upper Old Zoo Trail at a junction with the Bee Rock and Mineral Wells Trails. The Upper Old Zoo Trail winds back toward the trailhead through an especially picturesque stretch of oak trees. Ignore the prominent user trail at 1.1 miles, and it's smooth sailing and only a slight incline to 1.6 miles, then downhill from there. Keep left at the Fern Canyon Trail to return to the trailhead.

GO FARTHER

For an added challenge, you can also use this route to tackle Bee Rock (Hike 21)—but be warned that it's significantly tougher than the Old Zoo Loop, even though it's not much longer.

The tiny cages at the Old Zoo really give you an appreciation for how much zoos have improved.

21 BEE ROCK LOOP

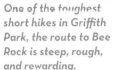

One of the toughest short hikes in Griffith Park, the route to Bee Rock is steep, rough, and rewarding.

Distance: 2.8 miles roundtrip
Elevation Gain: 730 feet
High Point: 1056 feet
Difficulty: Challenging
Time: 2 hours
Amenities: Water and restrooms at Old Zoo picnic area and near trailhead
GPS: 34.134551°N, 118.285678°W
Before You Go: Free Shakespeare Festival in the Old Zoo picnic area early some evenings in summer

GETTING THERE

PUBLIC TRANSIT Metro bus 96 and the Griffith Parkline stop at Griffith Park and Crystal Springs Drives. From there it's just a short walk west to the trailhead.
DRIVING From Crystal Springs Drive, turn west toward the merry-go-round at Park Center and drive through Lot One to get to Lot Two. A smaller amount of alternate parking can be found off Griffith Park Drive, just to the north.

An iconic route to one of the most prominent geographic landmarks in the park, this climb up to the top of Bee Rock is a fun but challenging scramble on one of its roughest official trails. Get ready to do a bit of bushwhacking and keep your eyes peeled for false user trails on this one—or you can take the easier alternate route that's described for the descent.

GET MOVING

Begin in the picnic area just to the north of Lot Two and head west on one of the paths toward the Old Zoo grounds. You'll climb up a paved path on a hill to reach a wide-open picnic area surrounded by the remaining portions of the Old L.A. Zoo. Explore the Old Zoo grounds if the mood should strike you (check out Hike 20 for more), or just follow the paved path to 0.3 mile, where you'll pop through an opening in the chain-link fence and keep to the left.

At this somewhat-confusing trail junction, look for the canyon heading west with the check dams in it—that's where the Bee Rock Trail heads, and it's where you should go, too.

The Bee Rock Trail is a little deceptive—it starts out looking like any other fire road trail in Griffith Park. It's broad, it's well maintained, and it's steep in parts but not *terribly* steep. Then at 0.5 mile, the road just sort of stops and you're left wondering what happened.

Look to the left, and you'll note a narrow, steep, single-track trail that climbs over a ridge and vanishes into the oak trees. This, folks, is the Bee Rock Trail. It's tough going, but it does offer up some very nice views of Glendale and the Verdugos through the sporadic tree cover. At 0.6 mile, keep to the right to continue climbing up.

It's two more steep, shrubby switchbacks on a trail that sometimes feels like it's not really a trail at all until you reach the final climb up, just before 0.8 mile.

The distinctive form of Bee Rock is visible from much of the eastern portion of the park.

There are some steps carved into the slope here, as well as some poured from concrete. Stay to the left once you reach the top of the ridge and follow the clear, fenced-in route to the edge of Bee Rock.

The chain-link fence that guards the edge of this rocky promontory is solid, but I wouldn't test it. And I certainly wouldn't try to climb over it either. Enjoy the views, don't fall, and return back along the ridge, skipping past the steps you climbed up to meet up with Vista Del Valle Drive.

Although you can do this hike as a quick out-and-back, the Bee Rock Trail can be a little messy on the descent. For a much easier time and a change of scenery, keep right to head west and then north on Vista Del Valle Drive to the Bill Eckert Trail at 1.2 miles, then keep right to descend back to the Old Zoo picnic area on that wide, gently sloped fire road.

GO FARTHER

I like to start out in Lot One and split the Old Zoo Loop (Hike 20) to make this a longer hike. That, combined with the descent on the Bill Eckert Trail, adds about an extra mile to the round-trip.

22 AMIR'S GARDEN

Enjoy a lush, irrigated garden that sprang from a firebreak through the spirit of American volunteerism.

Distance: 1.3 miles roundtrip
Elevation Gain: 410 feet
High Point: 810 feet
Difficulty: Easy
Time: 1 hour
Amenities: Restrooms and water at Mineral Wells picnic area and the Wilson and Harding Golf Courses Club House; water fountain, horse trough, and sometimes dog bowls at Amir's Garden
GPS: 34.145025°N, 118.293823°W

GETTING THERE

PUBLIC TRANSIT At the time of writing, there are no transit options for this hike.
DRIVING From Los Feliz Boulevard, head north on Crystal Springs Drive past Park Center and take a left on Griffith Park Drive. Pass the Wilson and Harding Golf Courses and driving range, and park near the southern end of the Mineral Wells picnic area at the intersection of Mineral Wells Road and Griffith Park Drive. There is also parking available along Griffith Park Drive here—just be wary of parking too close to the driving range lest your car fall victim to an over-enthusiastic golfer.

The last and arguably best cared for of the volunteer citizen gardens in Griffith Park, Amir's Garden is a beloved and iconic landmark hidden in plain sight. With an inspirational story and hand-built, meandering paths through surprisingly lush garden grounds, this is a must-visit destination for those who love the quieter side of Griffith. Tread lightly and slowly, and you may be inspired to volunteer here, too!

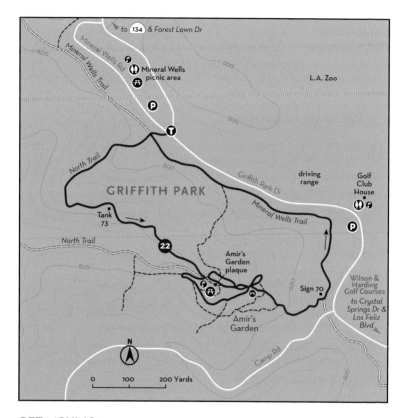

GET MOVING

A trek to Amir's Garden can be done one of two ways: as an easy fire road ascent with noticeable but relatively gentle incline or as a quick climb up one of two sets of rustic staircases that'll work up a sweat and *really tone those glutes*. The route as described here takes the easy way up and the steep way down, but you've got some options.

Head onto the North Trail from the south end of the Mineral Wells picnic area—it's the one climbing up the hill toward Tank 73. The trail rises through some of Griffith's iconic chaparral landscape. Laurel sumac, black sage, and monkeyflowers are abundant here, and the fluffy white flowers of bigpod ceanothus are one of the first signals of spring. In the early mornings you may also spot a coyote or deer making their way across the hillsides, too.

You'll round Tank 73 at 0.2 mile and start to see some spectacular views to the east, looking across the L.A. Zoo toward Glendale and the Verdugos and the San Gabriels. By the time you reach 0.4 mile, the landscape starts to get much more lush. Stay on the North Trail, and you'll soon reach the open picnic area of Amir's Garden. You'll spot a few picnic tables as well as a water fountain and a horse trough.

Amir's Garden is a mix of drought-tolerant and California native plants and succulents—and they're irrigated, too. That means that the garden is reliably green even when the rest of the park turns gold and brown in the dry summer months. The garden itself is a haphazard spiderweb of narrow, hand-built pathways and wooden staircases and—honestly—it's best experienced by just wandering around and seeing where you end up. If you don't want more detail, just know there are two stairways you can take back down to the Mineral Wells Trail—one you reach by generally heading north in the garden and the other you reach by generally heading east. There is a user trail that heads southwest toward Griffith Park Boys' Camp, but that camp is officially reserved for people participating in programs there.

If you want a *bit* of direction here, check out the picnic tables and plaque about Amir Dialameh, then cross to the southwest side of the ridge. Keep to the right, then take your first left to loop back toward the east. There are branches that head above and below this level, but staying on the track you're on will take you to the garden's eastern edge (ignore another user trail to the south at about 0.5 mile).

A bit farther on this level, just above a brightly painted bench, you can see one of the staircases down toward the Mineral Wells Trail. If you're ready to descend, you can take it—or you can hook back to the left to explore the garden's northern pathways. There are two levels of garden path to the north with a handful of hidden alcoves, benches, and hand-built garden planters, as well as another staircase heading down to the Mineral Wells Trail. You'll reach those stairs at around 0.6 mile, where you can descend or continue back east to that bright bench and the first set of wooden stairs you saw. A short spur to the north of that bench hits a dead end—don't try to continue past what is clearly the garden's border.

You'll start your descent around the 0.8-mile mark—and I'm warning you, it's steep. In the dry months, the dirt on these exposed slopes in Griffith Park can be pretty slippery, so take it slowly and only attempt this descent if your shoes have good grip.

If you're taking the stairs by the painted bench, you'll reach the Mineral Wells Trail at 0.9 mile at an unsigned junction just south of wayfinding Sign 70. Keep left to return to the trailhead, passing the upper parking lot for the Golf Club House. You'll pass the other descent route from Amir's at 1.2 miles and reach the trailhead at 1.3 miles.

23 MINERAL WELLS LOOP

This fitness loop in the north of the park serves as a great introduction to the trails beyond Amir's Garden.

Distance: 4.2 miles roundtrip
Elevation Gain: 1060 feet
High Point: 1270 feet
Difficulty: Challenging
Time: 1.5 hours
Amenities: Restrooms and water at Mineral Wells picnic area; water fountain, horse trough, and sometimes dog bowls at Amir's Garden
GPS: 34.145025°N, 118.293823°W

Need a quick break? Why not soak in some gorgeous views while you're at it?

GETTING THERE

PUBLIC TRANSIT There is no public transit access.

DRIVING From Los Feliz Boulevard, head north on Crystal Springs Drive past Park Center and take a left on Griffith Park Drive. Pass the Wilson and Harding Golf Courses and driving range, and park near the southern end of the Mineral Wells picnic area at the intersection of Mineral Wells Road and Griffith Park Drive. There is also parking available along Griffith Park Drive here—just be wary of parking too close to the driving range lest your car fall victim to an over-enthusiastic golfer.

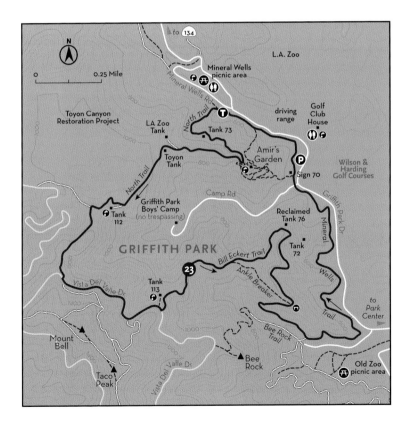

THE FIRE OF 1933

On October 3, 1933, more than 3700 men toiled inside Griffith Park building trails, roads, and landmarks as part of the Depression era welfare work programs. Despite a cool start to the morning, Santa Anas cranked the thermometer up to 100 degrees in downtown L.A.

A little after 2:00 PM, smoke was spotted rising above Mineral Wells Canyon near the Golf Club House, and workers building a road above the canyon descended to stamp out the fire with their shovels (it is still in dispute whether the men volunteered to go or were ordered to go).

The fire seemed small and under control, but by the time the Los Angeles Fire Department arrived, they saw a different disaster: 3000 untrained workers in a 40-acre fire area. Around 3:00 PM, the winds shifted, whipping the flames up the canyon walls. In a matter of minutes, a smoldering flare-up turned into a raging inferno that surrounded a huge number of people with no idea what to do for those conditions.

Due to the decentralized work system on the project, the death tolls from what became known as the Griffith Park Fire varied wildly . . . but the official death toll was set at 29 and a burn area of 47 acres. It remains the deadliest wildfire in Los Angeles history, and until the Camp Fire in 2018 it was the deadliest in California history, too. The cause remains unknown.

On the North Trail just west of Amir's Garden, look for 29 pine trees planted on the side of the trail in memory of those who lost their lives in this fire. A memorial plaque was installed nearby in late 2019.

Tucked behind the L.A. Zoo, the Mineral Wells picnic area maintains a lovely sense of peace and calm compared to the more crowded corners of Griffith Park. This trailhead is a popular starting point—but most hikers travel only up to Amir's Garden and back. If you keep trekking past that beautiful oasis, you can get a nice little workout, soak in excellent views, and in many places feel like you've got the entire park to yourself.

GET MOVING

From the south end of the Mineral Wells picnic area, cross Griffith Park Drive and head up the North Trail toward Amir's Garden. You'll pass Tank 73 at 0.2 mile and start to get some lovely views toward the north and northeast. By 0.4 mile, the chaparral and sage scrub of the lower elevations give way to the curated vegetation of Amir's Garden. Enjoy the shade or grab some water if you need it, then continue on the North Trail.

As you climb west on the North Trail, you'll pass the living memorial to those who perished in the Fire of 1933 (more on that in the sidebar) and head between the L.A. Zoo Tank and Toyon Tank. The North Trail hugs the south edge of the Toyon Canyon Restoration Project, and there's a short spur to Tank 112 (and a water fountain) at 0.9 mile.

Keep left at the unnamed trail at 1 mile to continue climbing to paved Vista Del Valle Drive, where you'll take a sharp left at 1.3 miles toward Bee Rock. Stay on Vista Del Valle, passing another water fountain and Tank 113 at 1.7 miles, then take a sharp left at 1.8 miles to descend on the Bill Eckert Trail.

The Bill Eckert Trail makes a winding, gentle descent, but if you're in the mood for a slight shortcut and a more rugged trek down, you can hop on Ankle Breaker at 2.1 miles. You'll hit the Mineral Wells Trail at the 3-mile mark, then keep left to head back to the Mineral Wells picnic area.

The Mineral Wells Trail is easy to follow and makes a few rolling ups and downs as it makes its way north. You'll cross Camp Road at 3.9 miles and pass one of the staircase routes to Amir's Garden just past Sign 70 and then another route up at 4.1 miles. You'll reach the trailhead shortly afterward.

24 TOYON CANYON LOOP

A surprisingly quiet and peaceful loop in the northern region of Griffith Park—even though it's near a landfill

Distance: 2.7 miles roundtrip
Elevation Gain: 700 feet
High Point: 1150 feet
Difficulty: Moderate
Time: 1.5 hours
Amenities: Restrooms and water at Mineral Wells picnic area; water fountain, horse trough, and sometimes dog bowls at Amir's Garden
GPS: 34.145025°N, 118.293823°W

GETTING THERE

PUBLIC TRANSIT There is no public transit access to this hike.

DRIVING From the 134, head south from the Forest Lawn Drive Exit and turn east onto Zoo Drive. In 0.2 mile, keep right at Travel Town to head onto Griffith Park Drive for 1.4 miles. This trail begins at the south end of the Mineral Wells picnic area, at the intersection of Mineral Wells Road and Griffith Park Drive.

This lightly traveled loop trail hits some of the most popular areas in the northern section of Griffith Park but somehow manages to provide some exceptional stretches of solitude along the way. Start out at the Mineral Wells picnic area—often bustling in the summer months—then wind along the outskirts of a canyon that was turned into a landfill (they thought it was a good idea at the time?) and descend through the landscape of some tragic human history into the beautiful oasis of Amir's Garden.

GET MOVING

From the south end of the Mineral Wells picnic area, cross the street and look for the North Trail. For now, you're going to keep to the right and follow the Mineral Wells Trail north as it parallels the paved road below. On quiet days, you have a good chance of spotting some wildlife here—both on the trail and up in the trees, too.

The reclaimed land at the Toyon Canyon Restoration Project was initially pitched as being usable as parkland by 1963.

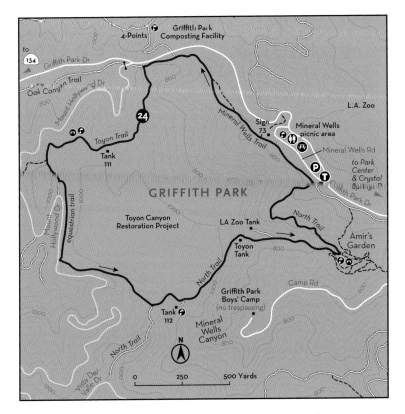

Just before 0.3 mile, pass a flood control dam and you'll get your first glimpse of the looming form of the Toyon Canyon Restoration Project—more on that later in a sidebar. It's an old landfill, but I promise it's nicer than it sounds. For now, keep left and follow the direction on wayfinding Sign 73 ("No Vehicle Access") toward Griffith Park Drive and the Rattlesnake Trail. The trail splits after the sign—a gravel path takes the high road while the low path is dirt. Both routes meet up again in 0.2 mile, so go low if you want a bit more time in the oaks or high if you want some better views of the landfill.

At 0.5 mile, the trail reaches the Griffith Park Composting Facility, and you may be wondering, "Why the heck is this guy taking me on a hike to landfills

ONE MAN'S TRASH

Visible from many sections of the northern side of Griffith Park is a large, barren, terraced landscape that seems out of place in the otherwise rugged terrain. Beneath this terraced hill lies the former Toyon Canyon.

By the 1950s, L.A.'s smog was becoming a problem that politicians couldn't ignore anymore. Although the science at the time was clear that auto exhaust was the primary cause of the city's smog, it was easier to outlaw trash incinerators instead. But what to do with all that garbage now? How about burying it under dirt?

The landfill idea began in England in 1912 and made it to California by 1937. In 1957, it came to the heavily vegetated Toyon Canyon, where the City Recreation and Parks Commission gave the green light to "development" of the canyon for recreation. Although today it might seem counterintuitive to put a landfill in the middle of a city park, at the time the commission was enthusiastic about manufacturing more flat land for park goers. The initial proposal featured parking and picnicking facilities atop the new landfill, along with basketball, volleyball, and tennis courts—all to be ready by 1963.

Few people at the time put up any opposition. One notable exception was Van Griffith, Griffith J. Griffith's son, who unsuccessfully sued the City over the plans. The landfill opened in 1958 and operated until 1985. Later recreational plans for the area included massive picnic areas, a nine-hole golf course, a youth hostel, and a 90-acre meadow. But as of 2019, the massive manmade slope is greened with hydroseed and is still not open to the public.

and composting centers?" Look, I get it—just trust me on this one. Also, if you're into gardening, this composting facility is a great source for free mulch. Residents can also purchase discounted composting bins and take free composting workshops here on the fourth Saturday of every month.

Keep to the left and look for the sign marking the start of the Toyon Trail. Start your steep climb above Griffith Park Drive, and keep left again at the Oak Canyon Trail to keep climbing up. Ahead, the trail is lined by blue gum eucalyptus trees and dense groves of black sage, which part to reveal Disney's and ABC's Burbank studios (and the Santa Susana Mountains if you're lucky) just over the ridges above Travel Town to the northwest. If you're hiking in the winter or spring, be sure to look to the north for stunning views of Glendale with the ridges of the Transverse Ranges behind it. Keen eyes may also spot old wooden signs for the Toyon Trail slowly fading among the trees.

By 0.9 mile the trail levels out on the north side of Toyon Canyon and passes Tank 111. At mile 1, there's a small bench and water fountain, and on the ridge just to the north of the trail here, you'll spot some faded signs noting the presence of Nevin's Barberry (*Berberis nevinii*), an endangered, endemic California native plant. Calflora estimates that only about 500 individual plants remain. You'll most easily spot the ones here in the spring, when bursts of yellow flowers appear amid their serrated leaves.

The trail turns south and loops around a facility that converts some of the landfill's methane gas into electricity. Keep left at 1.2 miles to head toward Vista Del Valle Drive on an equestrian trail that really is a mostly unmaintained path next to a maintenance road. After rains, this section can get pretty muddy.

Follow the trail as it makes a sharp east turn at 1.5 miles, paralleling Mount Hollywood Drive. This last little section hasn't been especially photogenic, but it's about to get nice again. And steep. Ignore the paved Mount Hollywood Drive and keep following an old road grade through the sage scrub as it makes a beeline up toward the North Trail. It's the steepest incline on the loop, but it also provides the best views of the landfill (again, I'm telling you—it's nicer than it sounds!)—both the sheer scope of it and what may *someday* be usable parkland again.

After a steep but short climb up, keep left to start a gentle descent on the North Trail. Pass the short spur leading to Tank 112 at 1.8 miles (there's a small picnic area and water stop there if you need them), and be sure to scan the hills southeast across Mineral Wells Canyon for the most improbable inground swimming pool you've ever seen (the pool is part of the Griffith Park Boys' Camp and is off-limits to the public).

At 2.1 miles, keep right to stay on the North Trail as it wraps around the north side of the Toyon Tank. Heading east on a ridge, you'll have more exceptional views east toward Glendale. Walk past the trees planted as a memorial to fallen firefighters (see The "Fire of 1933" sidebar) and you'll reach Amir's Garden at 2.3 miles. Enjoy the shade and history (learn more on Hike 22) and head down the North Trail to return to the trailhead.

25 NORTH PEAKS LOOP

A challenging adventure through the park's rugged backcountry and sometimes confusing interior.

Distance: 8 miles roundtrip
Elevation Gain: 2500 feet
High Point: 1614 feet
Difficulty: Very challenging
Time: 4 hours
Amenities: Water and restrooms along route
GPS: 34.155439°N, 118.303302°W
Before You Go: Northern park trails have high levels of equestrian traffic; yield on the trail and try not to make loud noises or sudden movements when they pass

GETTING THERE

PUBLIC TRANSIT The Griffith Parkline stops at Travel Town.
DRIVING From the 134, head south from the Forest Lawn Drive exit and turn east on Zoo Drive, then head south on Griffith Park Drive. There is a small dirt parking area just south of the Travel Town parking lot.

Like the Griffith Peaks Traverse (Hike 26), this is one of the most difficult routes in the park—primarily because it spends a good amount of time in the park's rugged, relatively quiet center. Unlike the traverse, though, this is a full loop route that doesn't need a car shuttle—and as it spends most of the time in the northern part of the park, it offers up more opportunities for solitude by avoiding the more crowded sections around the Hollywood Sign and Griffith Observatory. If you choose to make a full day of it, you'll *really* know the interior of Griffith Park when you're done.

GET MOVING

From the dirt lot south of Travel Town, cross Griffith Park Drive and head south on the Oak Canyon Trail. At 0.3 mile, keep right at the unsigned junction to head onto the Suicide Trail, which narrows and steepens considerably. By 0.5 mile, you're basically climbing straight up the side of a hill with increasingly great views. The Suicide Trail turns southwest at 0.6 mile and meets paved Mount Hollywood Drive just past the 0.6-mile mark. Turn left onto the road to briefly backtrack north, then hang a right onto the Toyon Trail at 0.7 mile.

Keep right at 0.9 mile to head south on a signed equestrian trail that skirts the southwestern edge of the Toyon Canyon Restoration Project and parallels Mount Hollywood Drive, and at 1.3 miles, keep to the left to follow an old road grade up to the North Trail, which you meet just before 1.5 miles.

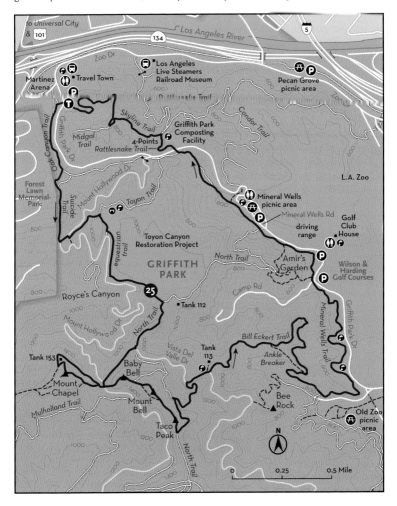

THE GRIFFITH PARK TEAHOUSE

In late June 2015, a number of journalists and writers around L.A. received a mysterious email invitation "for tea and wishes overlooking the city. Sun rise, Griffith Park." Once there, curious early risers followed a set of LED candles to rarely visited Taco Peak, where a collective of anonymous artists had—overnight—built a teahouse atop the footprint of an old utility shack.

The teahouse was constructed using redwoods killed in the 2007 Griffith Park Fire. Visitors could partake in a Japanese tea ceremony, ring a prayer gong, and leave wishes for the city on wooden placards (as we were in the middle of an extended drought, many of the prayer cards simply read "Rain"). The building was adorned with a carved griffin that was part red-tailed hawk and part P-22—the beast had a tracking collar.

The artists did not seek permission for the structure, so it was taken down several weeks later and donated to the city. It briefly went on display in San Pedro a year later but hasn't been seen since.

The artists branded themselves as the Art Department and can be found online at www.archivesandrecords.info. In 2018, they staged an immersive nighttime event with bioluminescent protozoa at the Griffith Park Boys' Camp—this time, they got permission.

The Griffith Park Teahouse was a short-lived but beautiful structure.

Stay right here to head south on the North Trail, and keep right again at paved Vista Del Valle Drive at 1.7 miles. Meet up with Mount Hollywood Drive at a wayfinding sign at 1.9 miles, and here's where the trail gets a little confusing for a bit.

From here, you'll be topping the four named peaks in Griffith Park's deep interior—Mount Chapel, Baby Bell, Mount Bell, and Taco Peak. To the west, Chapel is the first. Head south, then take a sharp right onto an unnamed fire road. You can see the faint and unsigned Mount Chapel Trail paralleling it for a bit—that's your return route. For now, keep to the fire road as it winds on the north side of Mount Chapel around Tank 153. At 2.3 miles instead of following another unnamed trail heading west, hike just behind Tank 153 and look for a

faint trail that heads directly to the summit of Mount Chapel, where you top out just before the 2.4-mile mark.

To descend, look for a "trail" heading east from the summit. It's very steep, rocky, and often slippery, so be prepared to use your hands to scramble or perform a graceful butt slide on certain sections (you'll be doing that a lot in this area of the park). You meet up with the Mount Chapel Trail at 2.5 miles and return to the paved section of Mount Hollywood Drive shortly thereafter.

Once you hit Mount Hollywood Drive, backtrack north and look for a narrow single-track trail on the east side of the road before you get to Vista Del Valle Drive. This rugged little route takes you up along a ridge through the dense oak woodland of a bump that's been nicknamed Baby Bell by local hikers. Head east from the summit at 2.7 miles to reconnect with fire roads just before the 2.8-mile mark.

The Suicide Trail is one of the most rugged established trails.

The official route to Mount Bell is just a few steps to the south along the fire road, but most hikers—even those trying *really hard* to stay on designated trails—will likely cross the fire road and follow a rough user trail that follows the ridgeline to the summit of Mount Bell. This trail can be tough going and, like the designated trail to Mount Chapel, requires some scrambling along the way, but the route forward is fairly clear. Reach the rocky summit just after the 2.9-mile mark, then carefully climb and/or slide down to the east to the fire road again at 3 miles and make a nearly direct cross to climb up the prominent firebreak to the summit of Taco Peak.

From the summit of Taco Peak, you'll see that the fire road you just crossed dead-ends at a small rest area just to the east of the summit. To continue, head slightly east from the summit and follow the single-track trail south to the broad North Trail and make a sharp turn left at 3.2 miles.

Past the 3.4-mile mark, take a sharp right onto a short, unnamed trail (longtime Sierra Club hikers refer to this as the Cardiac Trail), and take a right onto paved Vista Del Valle Drive at 3.7 miles. You'll pass a water fountain and a short spur trail to Tank 113. Just beyond the tank, take a sharp left onto the Bill Eckert Trail and follow this or Ankle Breaker down to the Mineral Wells Trail at 5.2 miles.

Take a left to head north on the Mineral Wells Trail, passing Camp Road at 6.1 miles. If you're in the mood for a break, you can grab water, a snack, a meal, or a beer at the Golf Club House—otherwise stay on the Mineral Wells Trail to the northwest corner of the Mineral Wells picnic area, where you keep left at 6.7 miles to head to the Composting Facility at 7 miles.

Cross Griffith Park Drive and take the Rattlesnake Trail to 4-Points at 7.2 miles, where you head west on the Skyline Trail. Follow the Skyline Trail back to the trailhead, ignoring the dead-end spur of the Midgal Trail at 7.4 miles.

GO FARTHER

If you want a little more distance and some good elevation gain on the return, consider taking the Condor Trail to the Skyline Trail just north of the Mineral Wells picnic area instead of hiking through the Composting Facility and along the Rattlesnake Trail. Follow the directions for Hike 28.

26 GRIFFITH PEAKS TRAVERSE

This tough one-way route summits every named peak of the park's southern ridgelines.

Distance: 7.6 miles one-way
Elevation Gain: 2120 feet
High Point: 1820 feet
Difficulty: Very challenging
Time: 4 hours
Amenities: Water on second half of route
GPS: 34.132149°N, 118.337899°W
Before You Go: This one-way hike does not return you to the trailhead; use a ride-share service to get to the trailhead

This is what passes for a trail in the park's rugged interior.

GETTING THERE

PUBLIC TRANSIT There is no public transit access to the start of the trail, although the trail ends at a stop for Metro bus 96 and the Griffith Parkline and a short walk from a stop for Metro buses 180/181 and Rapid 780.

DRIVING From the 101 northbound or Cahuenga Boulevard, head east on Barham Boulevard. Take a right onto Lake Hollywood Drive and stay on that road as it meanders through a residential neighborhood. At the signed intersection with Wonder View Drive, descend a hill toward the reservoir and park along the road, minding the parking restrictions.

If you're setting up a shuttle at the end of the route, you can park in the lot just to the north of the pony and train rides. From Los Feliz Boulevard, head north into the park on Crystal Springs Drive and the lots will be on your right.

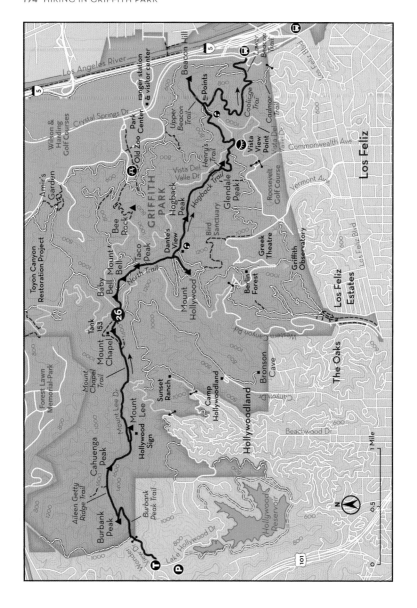

This exceptional route travels the entire length of Griffith Park from west to east, hitting every named summit on the easternmost ridgeline of the Santa Monica Mountains. This is the most difficult hike in this guidebook—the section between Mount Lee and Taco Peak is very rough and slow going, even for experienced hikers. But if you put in the effort (and keep your wits about you at numerous unnamed, unsigned trail junctions), you'll enjoy some of the most rugged terrain, stunning views, and surprising solitude Griffith Park has to offer.

GET MOVING

Follow the route described in Hike 3, kicking things off with a steep climb up the Burbank Peak Trail to the Aileen Getty Ridge Trail. Summit Mount Lee and snap some selfies with the tourists, then on your way back down, keep right before 1.7 miles to continue east on paved Mount Lee Drive. You'll be on the backside of Mount Lee here. To the north, you'll have views into the ever-expanding resting grounds of Forest Lawn Memorial-Park through some beautiful old-growth coast live oaks. To the south, look at the steep rock wall for resilient native plants who've carved out a home in this seemingly inhospitable environment—southern bush monkeyflower and California fuchsia put on showy displays in the late spring and early summer, while succulents like the lanceleaf liveforever look like creatures from another planet.

At 2.1 miles, your adventure truly begins (not to belittle the effort you've already made . . . but seriously, get ready). The single-track Mount Chapel Trail dives up into the oak woodland here at an unsigned junction. Keep left at the junction with a nearly vertical user trail nearby—they both end up on a ridge shortly. It's relatively smooth sailing heading east on the ridge toward Mount Chapel—you have a beautiful bird's-eye view of the Mulholland Trail below you, with eyelines to Mount Hollywood, the Captain's Roost, the Griffith Observatory, and Sunset Ranch. Hike east through dense growth of black sage, California buckwheat and brittlebush, and more monkeyflowers toward the looming figure of Mount Chapel—Tank 153 is visible on its northern flank.

At 2.4 miles, the Mount Chapel Trail curves to the right, dodging the summit on a mostly flat, very overgrown route. But you're on a summit-bagging adventure, so continue straight on an unnamed trail that basically makes a beeline right up the side of the mountain. It's rough, steep climbing that

Joe Klass and his friends brought an anti-establishment ethic to their trail runs. (photo by Teri Klass)

JOE KLASS AND THE TETRICK TRAIL RUN

Although Griffith Park maintains a healthy number of trail runners and official racing events, it seems safe to say none will ever approach the madcap nature of the storied Tetrick Trail Run, which was held in this corner of the park. The *very unofficial* race was organized by Joe Klass, head of the Griffith Park Athletic Club (a group of early morning weekend trail runners that's been described as "a pack of running anarchists"), and routed by fellow club member Bob Tetrick. The run's motto was simply "When in doubt, run uphill."

The run, like the club itself, was notable for its extreme irreverence—the race began with an arrow shot into the sky, mile markers were naked people holding signs with numbers, and before the award ceremony a man juggled a bowling ball, bowling pin, and active chain saw. Prizes were similarly nonsensical and changed year to year—one runner remembered a ceremony where the first-place winner got $10, second place got $20, all the way down to tenth place.

The Joe Klass Water Stop is named for Klass, who passed away in 2009. It's located at a favorite pit stop along the Tetrick Trail Run route. Tetrick passed in 2006.

The Tetrick Trail Run was part of a trend of antiestablishment runs meant to combat the rising registration fees and general stuffiness of racing culture. Unfortunately, once Griffith Park rangers found out about the nude mile markers, that was the end of their permits and the run . . . at least, it was *officially* the end of the run.

sometimes involves a bit of scrambling—get ready, that's kind of a theme on this route. Ignore a footpath before the 2.5-mile mark that hugs the northern slope of Chapel and meets a fire road near Tank 153—basically, you're just finding the ridge and staying on it until you reach the summit, which you'll hit just before the 2.6-mile mark.

The trail down isn't much easier—take your time and use the advanced hiking technique known as the butt-slide if the trail is too steep or slippery for you. Believe me, we've all done it. You'll meet up with the Mount Chapel Trail again at 2.7 miles, then join a fire road and meet up with the paved Mount Hollywood Drive at 2.8 miles.

Turn left to head north here and look for another narrow, unmarked footpath on the right-hand side of Mount Hollywood Drive before you reach Vista Del Valle Drive. Climb up here and loop back south to hit a ridgeline that takes you through dense brush to the unmarked summit of a bump lovingly named Baby Bell by local hikers. You reach the rocky summit just before the 3-mile mark. Follow the wooded trail southeast to the junction with three fire roads.

A very visible, very inviting user trail that continues toward Mount Bell straight ahead of you here will get you to the summit, but it's very rough and overgrown. Keep to the right instead to head southeast on the fire road toward Taco Peak, and look for a designated trail on the left-hand side of the road and take that instead. It's not *much* easier to follow, in my opinion, but it's the official route. You top out on Mount Bell just past the 3.1-mile mark, then descend on another very steep, very overgrown, very rocky trail where you will most definitely need to use your hands to scramble safely. Take it slow here—it's the last truly difficult section of trail on the route.

Make an essentially straight-line cross of the fire road at 3.2 miles to climb up a firebreak that is somehow an officially designated trail to the summit of Taco Peak. An octagonal platform and more incredible views await you at the summit at 3.3 miles. The descent from Taco Peak can be tough, too—you can follow a rough, steep firebreak south from the summit, or for a *slightly* easier descent, head east to meet the end of a fire road near some benches (and briefly the site of the Griffith Park Teahouse) and follow a rough footpath south to the North Trail at 3.4 miles.

Whew! Head south on the North Trail to the summit of Mount Hollywood (fun fact: this mountain was named Griffith Peak until the Colonel got sent to prison for a few years), which you'll reach at 3.8 miles, then backtrack and head east on the Hogback Trail at mile 4. Pass Dante's View (fill up on water here if you need it) and look for a short side trail at 4.3 miles if you want to stand atop Hogback Peak. The Hogback Trail heading east from here is a steep descent and can be deceptively slippery, so tread carefully. Ignore the user trails to the south and cross a small footbridge at 4.8 miles above Aberdeen Canyon. To bag Glendale Peak, keep left and take Henry's Trail to the summit at 4.9 miles, then backtrack and keep heading south on the Hogback Trail to Vista Del Valle Drive past 5.3 miles.

Head east on Vista Del Valle, and just before the Vista View Point, look for a broad, unmarked (again) path that climbs the hill toward Tank 114 (note: if you're short on water, head east on Vista Del Valle to the Joe Klass Water Stop to refill, then take the Upper Beacon Trail to 5-Points). This gentle, winding path wraps around the north side of Tank 114 through a lovely, quiet area of the park. If you're hiking on a Sunday, you might be able to hear the drum circle near the film office from here.

You'll reach 5-Points at 5.9 miles. Head straight to the summit of Beacon Hill on the Upper Beacon Trail, then backtrack to 5-Points and head south on the Coolidge Trail. Keep left at the Lower Beacon Trail at 7.1 miles and pass the Marty Tregnan Golf Academy, then keep right at the junction at 7.3 miles to cross Crystal Springs Drive and end up at the pony and train rides.

Buy yourself an ice cream or something. You deserve it!

27 RATTLESNAKE AND SKYLINE LOOP

This ridgeline hike in the northern part of the park offers up sweeping views and access to nearby attractions.

Distance: 3.2 miles roundtrip
Elevation Gain: 500 feet
High Point: 880 feet
Difficulty: Moderate
Time: 1.5 hours
Amenities: Picnic areas, water, and porta-potties along route
GPS: 34.155439°N, 118.303302°W
Before You Go: Northern park trails have high levels of equestrian traffic; yield on the trail and try not to make loud noises or sudden movements when they pass.

GETTING THERE

PUBLIC TRANSIT The Griffith Parkline stops at the Los Angeles Live Steamers Railroad Museum. Both the Parkline and Metro bus 96 stop at Riverside Drive/ Zoo Drive and at the Los Angeles Zoo, which are alternate places to start or stop your hike.

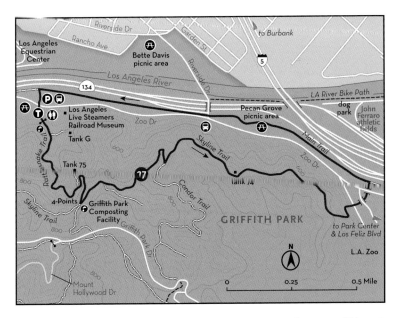

DRIVING From the 134, take the Forest Lawn Drive exit and enter Griffith Park on Zoo Drive. Keep left at Travel Town and head east on Zoo Drive. The trailhead is just outside the Los Angeles Live Steamers Railroad Museum. There are two small dirt lots and on-street parking available.

The Skyline Trail is aptly named—on this route exploring the eastern section of the trail, you'll have sweeping panoramic views of the region. On clear days, you can see all the way from the Simi Hills and Santa Susana Mountains across the San Fernando Valley and past the Verdugos and Glendale to the San Gabriels. And you'll be in the quieter northern part of Griffith Park where there are often more horseback riders than hikers.

GET MOVING

Just outside the main entrance to the Los Angeles Live Steamers Railroad Museum, look for the wide Rattlesnake Trail heading south into the foothills. Pass through the gate and check the posted map to get your bearings. There's

The Skyline Trail on the north side of the park is popular with equestrians.

a water fountain in the picnic area to your right if you need it, too. Otherwise, stretch out your legs and get ready for a climb!

The Rattlesnake Trail rises about 380 feet in just under 0.6 mile—and it really wastes no time doing it, either. Because you're on the north side of the ridge here, the trail stays a bit cooler in the morning—and there's a decent amount of shade here, too.

At 0.1 mile, ignore the side trail heading east (it leads to Tank G) and keep climbing. As you look to the north, you'll see the rough ridges of the Verdugo Mountains peeking up above the oak trees and sage scrub. In the late spring, look for showy orange and yellow monkeyflowers impossibly clinging to the steep walls near the trail. Year-round, you can spot the looming blue-and-yellow behemoth in Burbank to the north—North America's largest IKEA. Impressive, I know.

Keep climbing up the Rattlesnake Trail as the large green form of Tank 75 comes into view. A short spur trail leads to the tank at 0.4 mile, but keep on

HANGARS TO HOUSES

Back in 1912, the flat land where the parking lots for the L.A. Zoo and Autry Museum now stand would have looked very different. This was where Van Griffith built the Griffith Aviation Park—one of the first airfields in Los Angeles. At the time, this land was still technically part of the Griffith Reservation, land to be privately held by the Griffiths until the death of Griffith J. Griffith. His son, Van, envisioned an epicenter of aviation invention, production, and transportation.

That never really materialized, but the airfield definitely left its mark. William Boeing and Donald Douglas got their start here in a factory and flying school run by Glenn

Tiny Broadwick (State Archives of North Carolina)

Martin. In 1913, circus-performer-turned-aviation-pioneer Georgia "Tiny" Broadwick became the first woman to parachute from an airplane 2000 feet above Griffith Park. She later became the first woman to parachute into a body of water and the first skydiver to execute a planned free-fall descent; she also invented the rip cord. In 1914, Martin demonstrated an early airplane-mounted rifle, predating French pilot Roland Garros's machine gun–armed fighter plane by a year.

In 1924, the parks commission leased the airfield to the National Guard, which operated there until 1942. In 1946, the hangars were converted to emergency housing for returning World War II veterans as the Rodger Young Village, which housed up to 6000 veterans and their families in Quonset huts until 1954, when the village was razed. Today, the zoo and the freeway exchange between CA 134 and I-5 cover the site of the village.

climbing up and you'll reach the Skyline Trail just before 0.6 mile. At this staggered sort-of-four-way intersection known as 4-Points, you'll see an old water fountain and trough for the horses as well as some beautiful views of the interior of Griffith. You'll be able to make out the backsides of all the major peaks in the park as you continue on the Skyline Trail heading east—Cahuenga Peak, Mount Lee (the one with the radio towers), Mount Chapel, Mount Bell, Taco Peak, Mount Hollywood, Glendale Peak, and the drop-off at Beacon Hill, too.

You'll also make out the Griffith Park Composting Facility just below the trail to the south. To the north, you can see some sections of the Los Angeles River that resisted the concrete corset and support little islands of boulders and trees—a glimpse into the hopeful future of the rest of the river. The strange terraced incline to the south is the Toyon Canyon Restoration Project.

At the 1-mile mark, keep left to stay on the Skyline Trail heading toward the zoo. As you approach the zoo grounds, some large fences will begin to block your view to the south—but looking east you can soak in some spectacular vistas of Glendale, the Verdugo Mountains, San Rafael Hills, and San Gabriel Mountains. A 58-acre brush fire burned here in November 2018 at the same time the massive Woolsey Fire was wreaking havoc in the Santa Monica Mountains National Recreation Area. The fire was described as minor, but after the 2018–19 rainy season, recovery here looked fairly slow.

At 1.9 miles, the trail drops down to a zoo access road and it's not inherently clear where to go to keep hiking. Cross the paved access road and look for a dirt path that curves to the north—this is an equestrian connector trail that dips into a short tunnel to connect to the Main Trail, avoiding the need to try to cross Zoo Drive without a crosswalk.

Keep left at 2 miles to head west on the Main Trail. It's smooth sailing from here on out—a nice, flat, wide trail shared by walkers, hikers, runners, and equestrians. You pass some benches and picnic tables and a Recreation and Parks maintenance yard before returning to the dirt lot across the street from the trailhead.

28 OAK CANYON LOOP

A mostly gentle exploration in the quiet northern area with the chance to hear chimpanzees from the trail

Distance: 3.2 miles roundtrip
Elevation Gain: 710 feet
High Point: 880 feet
Difficulty: Moderate
Time: 1.5 hours
Amenities: Water on trail; restrooms at Mineral Wells picnic area
GPS: 34.153047°N, 118.308832°W
Before You Go: Northern park trails have high levels of equestrian traffic; yield on the trail and try not to make loud noises or sudden movements when they pass.

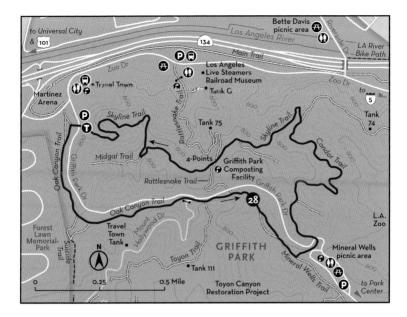

GETTING THERE

PUBLIC TRANSIT The Griffith Parkline stops at Travel Town.

DRIVING From the 134, head south from the Forest Lawn Drive exit and turn east on Zoo Drive, then head south on Griffith Park Drive. There is a small dirt parking area just south of the Travel Town parking lot.

If you're in the mood for a quiet time in the park but don't want to spend a ton of time on the trail, this loop through Oak Canyon is just what the doctor ordered. Featuring three solid inclines to get your heart pumping, this route offers pleasant shade from oak trees followed by full sun and exceptional ridgeline views. Hike this lightly traveled loop in the morning or evening for a good chance at spotting wildlife. Oh, and you'll almost *definitely* hear chimpanzees on this route, too. Seriously.

GET MOVING

Start at the small dirt lot just to the south of Travel Town (or if it's full, park in Travel Town). Head south on Griffith Park Drive and cross to the west side of the street to join the Oak Canyon Trail heading south. Enjoy this broad, shaded route as it parallels Griffith Park Drive. Ignore the unmarked junction with the Suicide Trail at 0.3 mile, and keep left at another junction with an unnamed connector trail just afterward.

Your first section of serious incline begins now. You'll cross Mount Hollywood Drive at 0.7 mile and stay straight at the junction with the Toyon Trail, reaching the Composting Facility at 0.8 mile. Keep to the right here to head toward Mineral Wells picnic area. The trail splits here—both routes take you to the same place: a flood control dam below the Toyon Canyon Restoration Project at 1.1 miles.

Keep left here to follow a faint footpath above the paved Mineral Wells Road, which keeps to the north of the picnic area. A faint user trail heads north from the sometimes-gated intersection with Griffith Park Drive and crosses the street at an "equestrian crossing" sign, which will put you on the Condor Trail at 1.2 miles.

Red-tailed hawks (Buteo jamaicensis) *perch in trees in and soar in the sky above Griffith Park.* (photo by Kat Halsey)

The Condor Trail doesn't mess around with elevation gain—you'll gain 200 feet in a little over 0.2 mile. But the steep climb is worth it. There's a good chance you'll be the only person around here. Birders will enjoy keeping an ear out for songbirds and watching hawks and falcons gliding overhead on thermals. If you bring some binoculars, you may also be able to see some of the birds in the L.A. Zoo from this trail—including some massive California condors. Your best views are around the 1.6-mile mark just before a locked zoo access gate.

The trail meanders north through an area that burned in 2018 at the same time as the Woolsey Fire in the Santa Monica Mountains National Recreation Area. The fire here was doused quickly, and although many oaks and laurel sumacs have resprouted, a lot of invasive black mustard has moved in, too. Hopefully the area will get some TLC soon.

Just before the 2-mile mark, keep left to head west on the Skyline Trail, where you'll get absolutely epic views of both the interior of the park and north toward the Verdugos and San Gabriels. Ignore the old fire road to your left at 2.2 miles, and stay on the Skyline Trail after you reach 4-Points and its water fountain just before 2.4 miles. Keep right at the Midgal Trail junction just before 2.7 miles, and the Skyline Trail will take you back to the trailhead.

29 ROYCE'S CANYON

Climb one of the steepest trails in the park to one of its most isolated canyons.

Distance: 3.4 miles roundtrip
Elevation Gain: 480 feet
High Point: 990 feet
Difficulty: Challenging
Time: 2 hours
Amenities: Restrooms at Travel Town near trailhead; water available near Toyon Canyon and at 4-Points
GPS: 34.153047°N, 118.308832°W
Before You Go: After a rain, give this area 1-2 days of sunny weather to dry out—hiking causes damage when trail is muddy. Northern park trails have high levels of equestrian traffic; yield on the trail and try not to make loud noises or sudden movements when they pass.

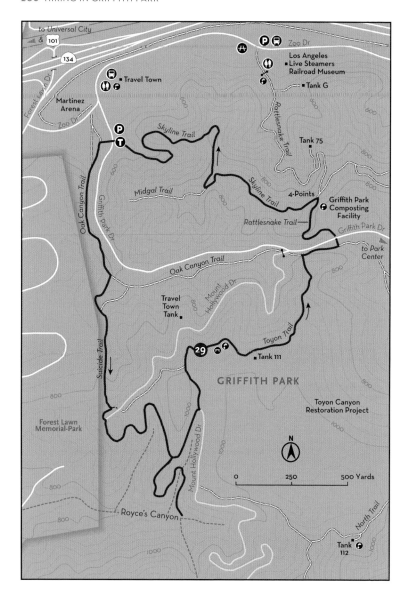

GETTING THERE
PUBLIC TRANSIT The Griffith Parkline stops at Travel Town.
DRIVING From the 134, head south from the Forest Lawn Drive exit and turn east on Zoo Drive, then head south on Griffith Park Drive. There is a small dirt parking area just south of the Travel Town parking lot.

Enjoy the rugged, quiet northern terrain of Griffith Park on this loop trail. Travel up one of the steepest routes the park has to offer before descending into a stunning canyon that was saved from becoming a landfill. Return back to the trailhead with views of what *could* have been in Royce's Canyon at the Toyon Canyon Restoration Project before taking in exceptional views along the Skyline Trail.

WHY IS THERE A GRAVEYARD IN GRIFFITH PARK?

Good question. And, as luck would have it, it's kind of a crazy story. The graveyards—technically there are two: Mount Sinai and Forest Lawn—are on land that was once part of Rancho Providencia. The parks commission had plans to purchase nearly 500 acres of the land north of Mount Lee to fold into Griffith Park after World War II. Unfortunately, the city was outbid by Glendale's Forest Lawn Cemetery Company.

A vicious public battle erupted, with opponents taking out newspaper ads warning about the dangers of having a graveyard upstream from a source of drinking water. Even Tina Griffith—Griffith's normally publicity-averse former wife—came out against the project. But the city council gave Forest Lawn the conditional permit in 1948 . . . and that's when things got *really* weird.

California has a state law that says that any ground with six people legally buried there is considered a graveyard permanently. Mike Eberts writes in *Griffith Park: A Centennial History*: "The corpses of six people who had recently died at the General Hospital were rushed to Rancho Providencia. The *Citizen-News* hustled two photographers and a reporter to the scene, where according to the newspaper's report, company employees threatened them with arrest if they set foot on cemetery property and tried to block the photographers from taking pictures of the hasty burials. Immediately afterward, a Forest Lawn spokesman announced that the burials converted the land to a cemetery, making further argument over the matter moot."

GET MOVING

This trail begins in a small dirt lot just to the south of the larger, paved parking lot for Travel Town. Head south along Griffith Park Drive and look for the signs marking an equestrian trail crossing the road. Hop across the road to the west side, then turn south on the broad Oak Canyon Trail.

This is a popular route into the park from the Los Angeles Equestrian Center across the L.A. River, so don't be surprised to share the trail with some friendly horseback riders. It's smooth sailing and a gentle ascent until the 0.3-mile mark. Keep right here at an unmarked junction to start on the Suicide Trail, which begins as a slightly steeper fire road winding through some lovely oak woodland before narrowing into a single-track footpath at the border of Forest Lawn Memorial-Park.

It's a bit of an odd experience, being on a trail called the Suicide Trail while literally looking at a graveyard (and perhaps a memorial service or two), but for those hikers who *don't* want to ponder their own mortality, just keep your eyes straight ahead. The trail climbs up through some dense but exceptionally beautiful sage scrub here—best experienced after winter rains have greened the hills a bit. Gooseberry, currants, and nightshades mix in with the usual black sage and California sagebrush, delighting the eyes and nose alike.

At 0.5 mile, the trail really throws the gauntlet down and makes a near-vertical beeline up the side of the hill. When you stop to take breaks—and you will—be sure to look back north toward Burbank and enjoy this shockingly rugged and lush terrain you've been climbing in.

The Suicide Trail turns southwest at 0.6 mile and levels out a bit at the fenced boundary with Forest Lawn. Follow the faint footpath to paved Mount Hollywood Drive and turn right to head deeper into the park. Just past the mile mark, look for the prominent sign for Royce's Canyon and follow the fire road down.

Few visitors ever make it to this most remote of trails in the most remote part of Griffith Park. If you've been exploring the rest of the park, you may be dumbstruck by just how rugged and wild it is. Dense oak scrub hugs a series of seasonal arroyos at the canyon floors, which can run wild with gurgling water in the wet season. To the north, a rounded rock face is punctuated with small caves and ephemeral waterfalls. And it's extremely quiet, too—when you reach the end of the road at 1.3 miles, consider having a silent snack break to see what wildlife reveals itself to you.

While you're enjoying this canyon, be sure to give thanks to the memory and determination of Royce Schaffer Neuschatz. As an L.A. County Parks and Recreation commissioner, she led the fight to prevent this area from becoming "Toyon II," an extension of the Toyon Canyon Restoration Project that looms in sight of Royce's. Neuschatz was a tireless champion of city parks in Los Angeles, even after she was ousted from her position for ruffling too many feathers at city hall—the lovely canyon you're in is named for her.

When you're done, backtrack to Mount Hollywood Drive and turn right, and at 1.7 miles keep left to walk on part of a paved driveway to the Toyon Canyon Restoration Project and toward the Toyon Trail. At 1.8 miles, keep left to hike up a short incline—on clear days in the spring, the reveal of Burbank and the Verdugos behind a grassy green meadow is not easily forgotten.

Keep right shortly after a quick descent to head toward Griffith Park Drive on the Toyon Trail along the northern boundary of the Toyon Canyon Restoration Project. Enjoy the interior park views and sometimes-steep descent,

If not for the efforts of Royce Shaffer Neuschatz and others, this area could have become a landfill.

and at 2.4 miles, cross the street at the composting facility to make one last climb up the Rattlesnake Trail. Keep left at 4-Points to head west on the Skyline Trail, and ignore the Midgal Trail at 2.9 miles. You'll have more beautiful views in every direction as you descend to the trailhead.

GO FARTHER

If you want to avoid the steep incline of the Suicide Trail, keep heading east on the Oak Canyon Trail at 0.3 mile and instead make your ascent on Mount Hollywood Drive.

30 MAYOR CRYER'S HIKE

Trace the (likely) footsteps of the first L.A. mayor to take an active interest in Griffith Park.

Distance: 4.8 miles one-way
Elevation Gain: 1400 feet
High Point: 1625 feet
Difficulty: Challenging
Time: 2.5 hours
Amenities: Water and restrooms along route
GPS: 34.121796°N, 118.296820°W
Before You Go: This one-way hike does not return you to the trailhead so use transit to return; limited parking and bus access during Greek Theatre events—check www.lagreektheatre.com for schedule.

GETTING THERE

PUBLIC TRANSIT The DASH Observatory shuttle and Griffith Parkline stop just south of the trailhead at the Greek Theatre. The DASH is accessible via several stops in the Los Feliz neighborhood and at the Vermont/Sunset subway station. **DRIVING** From Los Feliz Boulevard head north on Vermont Avenue for 0.7 mile. Parking here is limited to first-come, first-served lots. The trailhead is located on the east side of Vermont Canyon Road, just across the street from the parking lot north of the Greek Theatre.

After Griffith J. Griffith died in 1919, the City of Los Angeles finally began to pay attention to Griffith Park. L.A. mayor George Cryer was in office from 1921 to 1929 and oversaw much of the town's growth into a major city. Park historian Mike Eberts wrote that according to an interview with Van Griffith, the mayor loved Griffith Park immensely. Every Wednesday, he'd hike up Vermont Canyon, top Mount Hollywood, and then have his chauffeur pick him up near Crystal Springs in time for his afternoon meetings back in downtown. This route attempts to follow in his footsteps, although I can't guarantee there'll be a chauffeur waiting for you at the end of it.

GET MOVING

Full disclosure—the trail network in Griffith Park is a lot different than it was when Mayor Cryer was scrambling around in this area. The first trail to Mount Hollywood was authorized in 1909, but given the park's history of creating, losing, naming, and renaming trails, there's no way to *truly* know which way the mayor was hiking.

That said, this route takes you from where he started to where he ended before his afternoon meetings—and just a bit farther to a brand-new native plant garden commemorating the de Anza National Historic Trail.

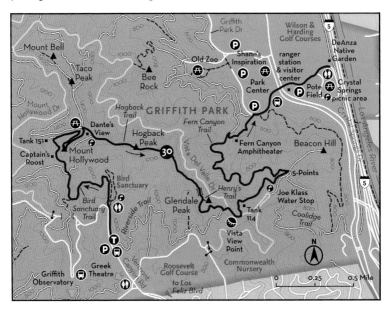

Hikers make their way up the Bird Sanctuary Trail.

From the Riverside Trailhead, hike north along Vermont Canyon Road past the bird sanctuary, then take a right onto the Bird Sanctuary Trail at 0.2 mile. Note that the Bird Sanctuary Trail is *not* the trail that takes you inside the actual bird sanctuary—it's the one that climbs up the ridge to its west.

At 0.7 mile, turn right and hike up the single-track trail to the Mount Hollywood Trail (not the rough user trail that makes an exceptionally steep route along the ridge itself). At 0.9 mile, you reach a four-way junction just below Mount Hollywood. Looking straight south, you can see the Griffith Observatory, which was still just a much-argued-about dream during Mayor Cryer's administration. Ignore the undesignated trail up the ridge and head west toward the Captain's Roost, then keep right at 1.2 miles to head to the summit of Mount Hollywood.

Soak in these exceptional views, then head north, keeping right at the Hogback Trail at 1.6 miles. Pass Dante's View (and fill up on water if you need it) and tread carefully on this steep decline to the footbridge near Henry's Trail. Stay on the Hogback Trail to the junction with Vista Del Valle Drive and the

Riverside Trail at 2.6 miles. Head south on Vista Del Valle Drive toward the Vista View Point and take a quick photo break if the skies are clear, then look for a fire road on the north side of Vista Del Valle that leads north around Tank 114. At the 5-Points junction at 3.2 miles, take a sharp left and follow the Fern Canyon Trail down toward Park Center, keeping right at 4.1 miles to take a more scenic route past the Fern Canyon Amphitheater and its native plant garden.

At 4.3 miles, stay on the equestrian trail heading east along the paved road to Lot One. Cross Crystal Springs Drive to join another section of equestrian trail near the ranger station and visitor center. Note the adobe building closest to Crystal Springs Drive—this is the last remaining building from the original Rancho Feliz. It currently serves as the Park Film Office, but the exterior walls date from 1853.

The equestrian route squeezes between the ranger station to the south and golf courses to the north before hugging the border of Pote Field and the edge of the Crystal Springs picnic area before ending at the Main Trail and the De Anza Native Garden at 4.8 miles.

31 MOUNT HOLLYWOOD FROM THE OLD ZOO

If you want to summit Mount Hollywood and avoid the crowds near the Observatory, this is the route for you.

Distance: 5 miles roundtrip
Elevation Gain: 1250 feet
High Point: 1625 feet
Difficulty: Challenging
Time: 2.5 hours
Amenities: Water and restrooms near trailhead; some water along route
GPS: 34.134551°N, 118.285678°W

GETTING THERE

PUBLIC TRANSIT Metro bus 96 and the Griffith Parkline stop at Griffith Park and Crystal Springs Drives. From there it is just a short walk west to the trailhead.
DRIVING From Los Feliz Boulevard, head north on Crystal Springs Drive. Turn west toward the merry-go-round at Park Center and drive through Lot One to get to Lot Two. A smaller amount of alternate parking can be found off Griffith Park Drive, just to the north.

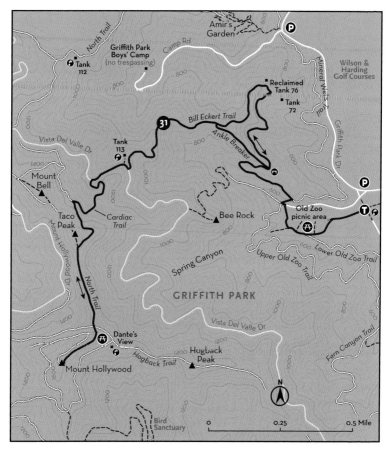

Summiting Mount Hollywood is a time-honored and special experience that every Griffith Park hiker should have . . . but sometimes coming up from any of the southern approaches can feel like an exercise in crowd tolerance, especially around the Griffith Observatory. This route avoids the crowds by starting in the east and coming up behind the summit on rarely used routes with fantastic views—you'll just have to pay a bit more attention at some unsigned trail junctions along the way.

Equestrians pass through dense California sagebrush atop Mount Hollywood.

GET MOVING

Start out in the picnic area just to the north of Lot Two. Head west on one of the paved or dirt paths that wind through the tables and barbecue pits made possible in part by the Land and Water Conservation Fund. Look for a wide paved path that winds up a low hill toward the Old Zoo—follow it to quickly reach a wide-open picnic area surrounded by remnants of the Old L.A. Zoo.

The Independent Shakespeare Co. performs here during the summer (see sidebar "Shakespeare Set Free"), but for most of the rest of the year, it's a place to hang out and climb around some surprisingly out-in-the-open, strange L.A. history. Keep to the left to follow the paved path along some of the Old Zoo infrastructure (more about that in Hike 20).

The looming form of Bee Rock (Hike 21) is especially majestic from here. Continue following the paved path as it circles around the Old Zoo grounds, and at 0.3 mile look for a small opening in the chain-link fence—it gets a little confusing here. Hop through the fence and keep to the left to hit the Mineral Wells Trail, then head right to start climbing up above the paved road. Keep left shortly afterward to climb up the Bill Eckert Trail, named for the legendary Griffith Park icon who started working as a gardener in 1949 and eventually wore badge #1 of Griffith Park's ranger unit from 1965 until his retirement in 1981.

At 0.7 mile, take a rough-looking ridgeline route near a picturesque bench. This is the Ankle Breaker route popular with the Sierra Club hikers, and it climbs through some dense and beautiful black sage, ceanothus, and laurel sumac. You'll also get some great views down at Amir's Garden (Hike 22) and the world-famous inground pool at the Griffith Park Boys' Camp. The Ankle Breaker rejoins Bill Eckert at 0.9 mile, so feel free to stay on Bill Eckert if you'd prefer a more gradual climb up.

Head west on the Bill Eckert Trail, and just after you pass Tank 113, keep right to head toward the North Trail on paved Vista Del Valle Drive at 1.3 miles, and at 1.4 miles look for a signed but unnamed path sometimes called the Cardiac Trail on the south side of the road that makes a steep, winding climb to the North Trail at 1.7 miles. Keep left to head toward Mount Hollywood's summit,

SHAKESPEARE SET FREE

Every summer, the Independent Shakespeare Co. takes up residence in the Old Zoo picnic area for several weeks to put on two plays by the Bard—one comedy and one tragedy—as the sun sets behind Bee Rock. The productions are lively and fun, and actors can frequently be found running through the audience. Watching Shakespeare performed with the occasional accompaniment of nearby coyotes and owls is a uniquely Griffith Park experience that's not to be missed.

The cast and crew put on a staggering number of performances, and each night is free. They do not accept reservations, picnics are welcome, and a concession stand sells snacks and hot and cold beverages. When the company first performed in nearby Barnsdall Art Park in 2003, their website notes the festival was "attended by 14 people and a dog," but by 2009 they'd outgrown Barnsdall and moved to Griffith, where they've performed for more than 40,000 since 2013. A permanent stage at the Old Zoo picnic area should be ready for the 2020 season. Head to www.iscla.org for a schedule (including the company's nonsummer, indoor productions in Atwater Village) and more information or to learn how to volunteer or donate.

ignoring the rough user trails to Taco Peak at 1.9 miles. Views of the interior of the park are exceptionally lovely here—and they're about to get better.

As you head south on an epic ridgeline toward Mount Hollywood, the rolling waves of Mount Lee and the Mulholland Trail come into view to the west. Eventually you'll start to see part of that famous sign, too. Keep heading south at the trail junction at 2.2 miles. You'll pass a small (and oddly, almost *always* empty) picnic area on the left and reach the summit of Mount Hollywood at 2.4 miles.

Snap photos, soak in the views, celebrate your climb, and hike back the way you came when you're done. I recommend taking the Bill Eckert Trail down instead of the Ankle Breaker to save a little wear and tear on your knees, but follow your heart!

GO FARTHER

For a longer loop route, head back down via the Hogback Trail (follow the directions for Hike 30 from Mount Hollywood to Lot One), then walk across the parking lot to the trailhead or take the Lower Old Zoo Trail back to the Old Zoo picnic area.

32 CUB TO CABOOSE

A tough but fun route that takes you across the entire park, from the south to the north

Distance: 5.1 miles one-way
Elevation Gain: 1370 feet
High Point: 1520 feet
Difficulty: Challenging
Time: 2.5 hours
Amenities: Water, food, and restrooms along the route
GPS: 34.108262°N, 118.307898°W
Before You Go: This one-way hike does not return you to the trailhead; use transit to return.

GETTING THERE

PUBLIC TRANSIT The DASH Hollywood stops at Franklin and Western Avenues. Metro buses 180/181, 207, Rapid 780, and the B Line subway stop at Hollywood Boulevard and Western Avenue. This trailhead is best reached by walking

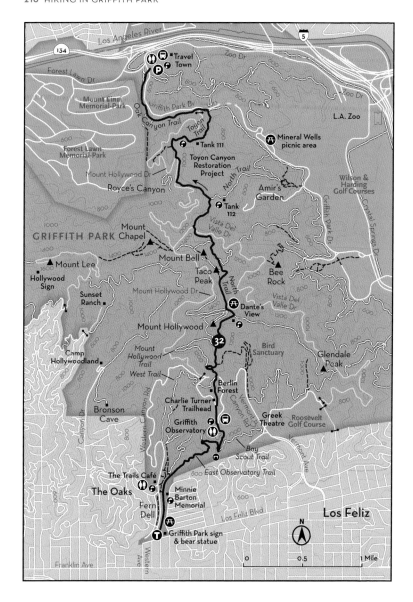

north on Western Avenue to the corner of Fern Dell Drive and Los Feliz Boulevard. The Griffith Parkline stops at the end of the route at Travel Town.

DRIVING From Los Feliz Boulevard, turn north onto Fern Dell Drive. Parking here can be tight as the day goes on, so either get started early or look for more parking near The Trails Café. Or leave the car at home on this one—it's easier!

Hike from an iconic statue at the southern tip of Griffith Park above and over the Santa Monica Mountains to a beloved (and free) transportation museum at the park's northern end. This epic route offers numerous opportunities for side trips and rest stops—and a great sense of accomplishment, too.

GET MOVING

This hike begins at the intersection of Fern Dell Drive and Los Feliz Boulevard, where a bear cub statue welcomes visitors to the southern entrance of Griffith Park (look for evidence of locals dressing him up a bit during certain holidays). Start by high-fiving the bear or shaking its paw, then hike north on the paved path that stays to the east of Fern Dell Drive. You'll pass a few picnic areas, Fern Dell Creek, and a water fountain memorial to Minnie Barton (see sidebar).

As you approach the playground at 0.5 mile, keep to the right to hike up the East Observatory Trail to Griffith Observatory, which you'll reach at 1.2 miles. Pass the *Astronomers Monument* and navigate across the observatory parking lot to the Charlie Turner Trailhead. Hike north through the Berlin Forest at 1.5 miles. Keep straight at the junction with the West Trail to continue toward Mount Hollywood.

Right after you cross over the tunnel for Vermont Canyon Road, you'll see a few different trails departing from the north side. Look for an unmarked trail with some steps cut into the stones to travel on a rugged and fun single-track trail that cuts off a bit of distance. If you find yourself hugging a metal pipe or scrambling up steep, dangerous slopes, you've gone on a user trail instead— the route you want to follow is tougher than the fire roads you've been on so far, but it's not technical.

At 1.7 miles, keep left at the junction with the Bird Sanctuary Trail to head north toward Mount Hollywood, and at 1.9 miles keep right to head toward

Dante's View on the Mount Hollywood Trail. Keep left at the viewpoint at 2.2 miles, and take a right to hike north on the aptly named North Trail just afterward (or take a short side trip to the summit of Mount Hollywood if you're in the mood!).

Stay on the North Trail to Vista Del Valle Drive, ignoring the Taco Peak Trail on the left at 2.5 miles, an unnamed trail to Vista Del Valle Drive on the right at 2.7 miles, and a trail toward Mount Bell at 2.8 miles. Cross Vista Del Valle at 3 miles and descend on the dirt North Trail until the 3.2-mile mark, where you'll veer left down an old dirt road toward the Toyon Canyon Restoration Project while hiking through fragrant sagebrush and enjoying incredible views of the Verdugo Mountains to the north.

Pass some buildings on the Toyon Canyon Restoration Project on a foot-path that parallels Mount Hollywood Drive. After a sharp turn north, join the paved road and keep right at 3.7 miles to head north toward the power produc-tion area of Toyon Canyon. Keep left just before you enter the off-limits area and follow an equestrian trail over a hill, then hop onto the Toyon Trail toward Griffith Park Drive by keeping right at 3.8 miles to continue your descent. At 4.3 miles, keep left to head west on the Oak Canyon Trail—a lovely, forested route that parallels Griffith Park Drive until it reaches Travel Town at 5.1 miles.

The Berlin Bear gives solid high-fives.

THE GOOD WORK OF MINNIE M. BARTON

The Minnie M. Barton Memorial is an ornate and somewhat spooky-looking tiered stone picnic area with a few water fountains just to the east of Fern Dell. A small plaque tells you the area was designated in July of 1947 by the Soroptimist Club of Los Angeles. Nothing at the site, however, tells you anything about Barton or what a Soroptimist is.

Barton was born in 1881 and moved to the then-boomtown Los Angeles from Kansas. By the turn of the century, she was leading a one-woman crusade to help destitute women who struggled with addiction and often turned to prostitution. She became the Los Angeles Police Department's first female parole officer in 1906 (and only the second female officer in the department). She founded the Big Sister's League in 1917 and raised funds for a halfway home in 1918 and a larger campus for women with children in 1923.

Barton was an outspoken and popular figure who never stopped fighting for poor women and children in Los Angeles. She passed away in 1946, and in 1947 the Soroptimist Club—an organization for businesswomen to help improve the lives of women and girls—honored her with this plaque. The Big Sister's League continued, changing its name to Children's Institute International in 1980. The institute currently provides medical and counseling services to at-risk youth and families at seven campuses throughout Los Angeles.

The Minnie M. Barton Memorial near Fern Dell

33 3-MILE TRAIL

Leave the car at home for this route that starts and ends at shuttle stops— and enjoy some less crowded Hollywood Sign views and spectacular sunsets.

Distance: 3.5 miles one-way
Elevation Gain: 600 feet
High Point: 1625 feet
Difficulty: Moderate
Time: 2 hours
Amenities: Water and restrooms along route
GPS: 34.120855°N, 118.300380°W
Before You Go: This one-way hike does not return you to the trailhead, so use transit to return; trailhead lot parking is limited during free hours and strictly enforced during paid hours—go early, take the DASH Observatory shuttle, ride Griffith Parkline, or hike in.

GETTING THERE

PUBLIC TRANSIT DASH Observatory and Griffith Parkline stops mark the beginning and end of this route and are highly recommended for transportation if you're not hiking in. Start at the observatory parking lot stop, and when you're done, pick up the DASH shuttle at the Mount Hollywood Drive and Western Canyon Road stop to return. The DASH Observatory connects with the DASH Los Feliz, several bus lines, and the Metro B Line subway.

DRIVING From Los Feliz Boulevard, head north on Fern Dell Drive, Vermont Avenue, or Hillhurst Avenue. It's paid parking at the observatory and along nearby roads from noon to 10:00 PM on weekdays and 10:00 AM to 10:00 PM on weekends, and it's expensive—$8 an hour. Really, don't drive here unless that's your only option.

You may ask yourself, "Hey, why is the 3-Mile Trail 3.5 miles long?" But while you're hiking this route, you're more likely to be distracted by the several exceptional viewpoints of the Hollywood Sign and the fact that you can get to and from this trail without ever setting foot in a private car. For those visitors who want to see the sign, this is one of the best options for moderate hiking— you'll get away from the observatory crowds at the official viewpoint and feel like a total park insider, too!

Mount Hollywood is a stunning place to watch the sun set over the Santa Monica Mountains.

GET MOVING

This little Hollywood Sign–spotting adventure begins at the parking lot drop-off for the DASH Observatory shuttle. Wander up to the overlook for the Hollywood Sign near the restrooms, but don't spend too much time—it's super crowded and you're going to get *much* better views on this route. Head to the north side of the parking lot to the Charlie Turner Trailhead. Fill up water if you need to, check out the plaque for Mr. Turner—the "Honorary Mayor of Griffith Park" and "Keeper Emeritus of Dante's View"—and the George Harrison memorial tree (actually the second, after the first was killed by, of all things, a beetle infestation), and then head north toward the Berlin Forest.

The wide stretch of fire road here on the Mount Hollywood Trail is a great place to look for love-seeking tarantulas around sunset during the fall. Look for the large but harmless spiders on the trail, or listen for the screaming European tourists. You'll quickly reach the Berlin Forest at 0.2 mile, where a quieter view of the sign awaits.

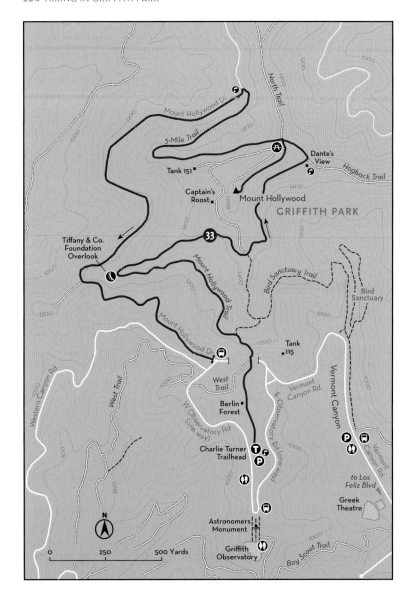

North Trail

Mount Hollywood Dr

3-Mile Trail

Tank 151

Dante's View

Hogback Trail

Captain's
Roost

Mount Hollywood

GRIFFITH PARK

33

Tiffany & Co.
Foundation
Overlook

Mount Hollywood Trail

Bird Sanctuary Trail

Bird
Sanctuary

Mount Hollywood Dr.

Tank
115

Western Canyon Rd

West Trail

West
Trail

Berlin
Forest

W Observatory Rd
(one way)

E Observatory Rd (one way)

Vermont
Canyon Rd

Vermont Canyon

Vermont Canyon Rd

Charlie Turner
Trailhead

T
P

P

to Los
Feliz Blvd

Greek
Theatre

N

0   250   500 Yards

Astronomers'
Monument

Griffith
Observatory

Boy Scout Trail

Keep heading north on the Mount Hollywood Trail, following a quick descent and junction with the West Trail at 0.3 mile. Cross over the traffic stuck in the tunnel below you and stay on the wide Mount Hollywood Trail as it wiggles toward the west, reaching the Tiffany & Co. Foundation Overlook at 0.7 mile, your next sign viewpoint.

The Mount Hollywood Trail makes a sharp turn east and climbs to a four-way junction at the 1-mile mark. Stay straight to loop counterclockwise to Mount Hollywood via Dante's View—you can go either direction but it's a gentler incline this way and there's a water fountain, too. Reach Dante's View and take a left on the Hogback Trail at 1.3 miles and another left at the signed memorial for fallen Los Angeles Police Department officer Jeffrey B. Lindenberg for a quick side trip to the summit of Mount Hollywood—I mean, you're *right there*, you know?

After you've viewed the sign again from the summit, backtrack to the LAPD memorial and head west on the 3-Mile Trail. This junction can be a little confusing—if you've come upon Tank 151, you've taken the wrong turn.

The 3-Mile Trail winds down a fire road to Mount Hollywood Drive, meeting the closed-to-cars pavement at 2.3 miles at an oddly manicured picnic area, where you'll turn south on Mount Hollywood Drive. Here, you'll be sharing the road with cyclists and runners and following the route of a short-lived shuttle program that attempted to ship some of the camera-toting tourists from the observatory to some other Hollywood Sign viewpoints to alleviate traffic and crowding. But all that shuttle seemed to do was anger cyclists who were enjoying a rare car-free L.A. road and conservationists who saw fragile terrain overrun by tourists cutting user trails and leaving trash around. So now you get to enjoy those views with none of the crowds—lucky you!

There are solid views along this entire road, but there's a great one at 3.1 miles. Continue down Mount Hollywood Drive to the hike's end at the DASH Hollywood stop just before the tunnel you passed over near the beginning of the hike.

GO FARTHER

If you don't want to take the DASH back to the trailhead but also don't want to drive in, consider parking at Western Canyon Road and hiking up. Combining this trail with Hike 10 forms a nice, longer loop.

Acknowledgments

Writing the first-of-its-kind guidebook for any area would be daunting, but doing so for a park as complex, complicated, and beloved as Griffith was definitely a challenge. This process would have been immeasurably more difficult if not for the following wonderful people:

Griffith Park's superintendent Joe Salaices was a tremendous help in getting this project started and moving in the right direction, not to mention a wonderful person to bounce grand ideas about the park off of. At his office, the incomparable Tracy James was my stalwart navigator through the park's community and always knew the next person I should talk to. I honestly could not have written this book without them.

Similar thanks go to Los Angeles City councilmember David E. Ryu and his staff, especially Catherine Landers, Shannon Prior, and Mark Pampanin. More elected officials should have meetings on hiking trails.

Griffith Park is a treasure trove of stories at least a mile deep. There is no better starting point to those stories than Mike Eberts and his books on the park.

It just so happened that this project coincided with an exceptional exhibit on the park's history at the Autry Museum of the American West. The staff at the museum have been absolutely heroic, especially Dr. Carolyn Brucken, Josh Garrett-Davis, Karimah O. K. Richardson, Chris Dzialo, and Ben Fitzsimmons.

Many thanks to April Spurlock and Jamie Pham at the Los Angeles Zoo; Bonnie Winings from Friends of the Observatory and Jennifer Wong from the Griffith Observatory; and Nancy Gneier of Travel Town. Thank you to Julia Bogany of the Tongva Tribe for her time and her land acknowledgment for the book.

Lynn Brown provided some exceptional information on the equestrian side of Griffith Park as well as a number of wonderful cowboy tales; Kris Sabo shared tons of stories, countless old maps, and invaluable insights on the park and its players; Teri Klass provided some fantastic anecdotes from her father's rogue-running past, a number of which I have sworn to keep secret. Phil Leirness and Lily Leirness of the Los Angeles Breakfast Club shared some early Leif Erikson Day programs and helped keep me in love with L.A. every Wednesday morning at club meetings—ham and eggs forever! Thanks to Kat Superfisky

OPPOSITE: *A hiker climbs Ankle Breaker.*

and Kathryn Pakradouni of Grown in LA for taking me behind the scenes at the Commonwealth Nursery and sharing their inspiring native plant dreams.

For sharing their trail knowledge and park expertise, thanks to Emmy Goldknopf from the Sierra Club and to Gerry Hans, Marian Dodge, and Kathryn Louyse of the Friends of Griffith Park. Thanks to Lauren Grabowski for helping me navigate the complicated name changes Metro is embarking on. Thanks to Nathan Masters for asking me to join him on horseback for a Griffith Park episode of *Lost L.A.* and to Angela Boisvert, Kathy Kasaba, Sasheen Artis, and Kathryn Noonan for dealing with my complicated schedule to make it happen.

When it comes to naturalist stuff, I'm more of a plants than animals guy, so extra-special thanks go to Miguel Ordeñana for sharing his P-22 photos and knowledge. The following fine photographers offered up images of critters I am too slow to snap: Sarah Brewer, Robin Black, Sheri Cohen, Marcus England, Kat Halsey, Kolby Kirk, Raphael Mazor, and Angela Serate.

Sienna DeGovia deserves credit for coining the Cub to Caboose route, Micha and Adelaide Boxer deserve credit for making my explorations of the Old L.A. Zoo much more fun, and Rian Kountzhouse deserves thanks for joining me at Travel Town on a surprisingly rainy day and for buying me some excellent diner food after I hiked to the old trains from my apartment in East Hollywood. I also have to thank Cameron Abdo for saying "yes" when I asked him if he wanted to try to hit sixteen different Hollywood Sign viewpoints in a day, even though I couldn't accurately tell him how long the hike would be or how hot it would get.

Thanks to Kate Rogers at Mountaineers Books for believing that a single city park deserved the in-depth guidebook treatment, and thanks to my project editor Laura Shauger and copyeditor Ali Shaw for making sure all my i's were dotted and t's were crossed.

For their inspiration and support, thanks to my fellow guidebook authors Shawnté Salabert and Scott Turner, and to Alissa Walker and Jenna Chandler of Curbed LA, Lila Higgins and Gregory Pauly of the Natural History Museum of Los Angeles County, and Beth Pratt-Bergstrom of the National Wildlife Federation. Thanks as always to the readers of Modern Hiker for keeping me going.

Finally, thanks to my partner, Daniel Lyman, whose encouragement and understanding have allowed me to make these guidebook dreams a reality. And thanks to our pit bull, Emmy, for reminding me to take breaks from writing, because dog bellies don't rub themselves.

Appendix I: Outdoor Advocacy and Volunteer Groups

California Native Plant Society—
Los Angeles/Santa Monica Mountains Chapter
www.lasmmcnps.org

Citizens for Los Angeles Wildlife
www.clawonline.org

City of Los Angeles Department of Recreation and Parks
www.laparks.org

Community Nature Connection
www.communitynatureconnection.org

Friends of Griffith Park
www.friendsofgriffithpark.org

Friends of the Los Angeles River
https://folar.org

Grown in LA
www.growninla.org

Latino Outdoors
http://latinooutdoors.org

Los Angeles Conservation Corps
www.lacorps.org

Los Angeles Parks Foundation
www.laparksfoundation.org

Nature for All
https://lanatureforall.org

Sierra Club Angeles Chapter
https://angeles.sierraclub.org

Theodore Payne Foundation for Wild Flowers & Native Plants
www.theodorepayne.org

TreePeople
www.treepeople.org

The Trust for Public Land
www.tpl.org

The Wilderness Society
www.wilderness.org

Appendix II: Recommended Media Resources

If you're interested in learning more about Griffith Park, L.A. history, or the out-doors around Los Angeles in general, here are some things I would absolutely recommend you check out. And because folks tend to just glaze over when these things are listed like a bibliography or works cited page, I'm going to try a different approach.

If you came here for hiking and want more, you should check out my other book, **Day Hiking Los Angeles** (2016), also published by Mountaineers Books, which features 125 trails all around the L.A. area. You should also visit the website I founded, **Modern Hiker** (www.modernhiker.com), which has hundreds of trails all across the American West as well as a lot of news, opinion pieces, and more fun writing from me. I mean, you made it *this* far, so I'll assume you like it.

If history is your thing and you want more Griffith Park stories, there are a ton of them, and nobody tells them better than Mike Eberts. Track down **Griffith Park: A Centennial History** (1996) and the companion e-book **Griffith Park: The Second Century** (2015). In 2019, KCET produced an episode of **Lost L.A.** on Griffith Park featuring Eberts, me, and L.A.'s historian-impresario Nathan Masters. The episode is called "Griffith Park," and you can find it at www.kcet.org/shows/lost-la. KCET also coproduced a series called **Tending Nature** with the Autry Museum as part of its **California Continued** exhibit. The show brings that exhibit's indigenous Californian stories to life. You can watch episodes at www.kcet.org/shows/tending-nature. The series takes its name from the book **Tending the Wild: Native American Knowledge and the Management of California's Natural Resources** (2013) by M. Kat Anderson.

I would also recommend trying to track down a copy of Griffith J. Griffith's book **Parks, Boulevards, and Playgrounds** (1910). It really gives you tremendous insight into Griffith's park philosophy and the ongoing conflicts Los Angeles has between private property and public parks. It's also a surprisingly fun read, especially once you know the park a bit. Right now you have to book time in the Rare Books Room of the L.A. Central Library to read it, but there are efforts to digitize the book for easier access.

The popular *Images of America* book series features a *Griffith Park* edition (2011) by E. J. Stephens and Marc Wanamaker that has tons of wonderful archival images of Griffith Park. Similarly, Greg Williams's *The Story of Hollywoodland* (1992) provides a point of view from the neighborhood that's surrounded by the park.

If you want to know more about the plants and animals you're seeing, the Natural History Museum of Los Angeles County published an incredible book called *Wild LA: Explore the Amazing Nature in and Around Los Angeles* (2019) by Lila M. Higgins and Gregory B. Pauly with Jason G. Goldman and Charles Hood. I would also recommend *California Plants: A Guide to Our Iconic Flora* (2018) by Matt Ritter; *Birds of Southern California* (2012) by Kimball L. Garrett, Jon L. Dunn, and Brian E. Small; and *The California Naturalist Handbook* (2013) by Greg de Nevers, Deborah Stranger Edelman, and Adina Merenlender. If you're interested in kicking off your own native garden, check out *California Native Gardening: A Month-by-Month Guide* (2012) by Helen Popper. If you're a fan of P-22—and who isn't?—you'll want to get your hands on Beth Pratt-Bergstrom's *When Mountain Lions Are Neighbors: People and Wildlife Working It Out in California* (2016) and track down Tony Lee's documentary *P-22: The Cat That Changed America* (2017).

If you're in the mood to get a better grasp and perspective around the city of L.A. and its relationship with the land, I have found the following books to be tremendously insightful, fun, and thought provoking:

- *After/Image: Los Angeles Outside the Frame* (2018) by Lynell George
- *Cadillac Desert: The American West and Its Disappearing Water* (1993) by Marc Reisner
- *City of Quartz: Excavating the Future in Los Angeles* (2006) by Mike Davis
- *The Control of Nature* (1989) by John McPhee

- *Finding Los Angeles by Foot: Stair, Street, Bridge, Pathway and Lane* (2014) by Bob Inman
- *LAtitudes: An Angeleno's Atlas* (2015), edited by Patricia Wakida
- *Secret Stairs: A Walking Guide to the Historic Staircases of Los Angeles* (2010) by Charles Fleming
- *This Is (Not) L.A.: An Insider's Take on the Real Los Angeles* (2018) by Jen Bilik with Kate Sullivan

Mr. Griffith welcomes guests to the park.

Index

About the Author

Casey Schreiner has been a leading figure in the Los Angeles hiking scene since 2006, when he founded the site Modern Hiker (www.modernhiker.com). Since then, the site has grown to become the most-read hiking website on the West Coast, breaking national news about public lands vandals and offering in-depth trail guides and reporting on outdoor issues facing the West.

Schreiner's first book, *Day Hiking Los Angeles* (Mountaineers Books), is the most up-to-date hiking guidebook for the Los Angeles area. In 2018, he was recognized by the United States Congress for his work connecting communities to the outdoors. He was also a speaker at the 2018 Outdoor Blogger Summit on the topic of social media and the outdoors, where his writing won the Best Advocacy Piece award. He sits on the advisory board of Nature for All and the Los Angeles Breakfast Club.

An award-winning writer, producer, and presenter, Schreiner has worked in television, live events, streaming programming, and interactive virtual reality programming for more than fifteen years. He lives with his partner, Daniel, and their pit bull, Emmy, and splits his time between East Hollywood, California, and Portland, Oregon. He is also surprisingly bad at camp cooking.

MOUNTAINEERS BOOKS, including its two imprints, Skipstone and Braided River, is a leading publisher of quality outdoor recreation, sustainability, and conservation titles. As a 501(c)(3) nonprofit, we are committed to supporting the environmental and educational goals of our organization by providing expert information on human-powered adventure, sustainable practices at home and on the trail, and preservation of wilderness.

Our publications are made possible through the generosity of donors, and through sales of more than 700 titles on outdoor recreation, sustainable lifestyle, and conservation. To donate, purchase books, or learn more, visit us online:

MOUNTAINEERS BOOKS
1001 SW Klickitat Way, Suite 201 • Seattle, WA 98134
800-553-4453 • mbooks@mountaineersbooks.org
www.mountaineersbooks.org

An independent nonprofit publisher since 1960

 Leave No Trace strives to educate visitors about the nature of their recreational impacts and offers techniques to prevent and minimize such impacts. Leave No Trace is best understood as an educational and ethical program, not as a set of rules and regulations. For more information, visit www.lnt.org or call 800-332-4100.